GRADES 1-3 READING COMPREHENSION

USING GRAPHIC ORGANIZERS TO TEACH LITERAL, INFERENTIAL, AND CRITICAL COMPREHENSION

Written by
Debra Flores, Alyssa Moran, and Tracey Orzo

Editor: Pamela Jennett

Illustrator: Ann Iosa

Cover Illustrator: Rick Grayson

Designer: Moonhee Pak

Cover Designer: Barbara Peterson

Art Director: Tom Cochrane

Project Director: Carolea Williams

Table of Contents

Introduction

Reading comprehension is the mind's ability to understand the ideas in a text and the message and purpose of the author. *Reading Comprehension 1–3* provides lessons that use specific genres to teach reading comprehension strategies. Teaching comprehension in a primary classroom is often seen as secondary to the instruction of decoding skills. If students are to become fluent readers who comprehend what they read, reading comprehension needs to be taught explicitly and consistently, starting in the early elementary grades.

Good readers are familiar with a variety of genres. Therefore, the comprehension skills in *Reading Comprehension 1–3* are genre-based. Good readers recognize how the indicators of specific genres, such as the captions and diagrams in nonfiction, or the problems and clues in a mystery, aid and assist them in deriving meaning from the text they read.

Good readers use a combination of six skills that lead to "real" comprehension:
Skill 1: Decoding—decode text fluently by integrating cueing systems: visual, meaning, and semantic.
Skill 2: Literal Comprehension—recall literal events, facts, or information that are explicitly stated in text.
Skill 3: Inferential Comprehension—integrate knowledge of the reader's world and literal information of the text to gain a deeper understanding of its story elements.
Skill 4: Critical Comprehension—extend and develop an understanding of text through discussion, comparison, classification, alteration, or imagination, thereby creating new views and knowledge.
Skill 5: Vocabulary—determine familiar and unfamiliar vocabulary.
Skill 6: Grammar—understand and use the grammatical, mechanical, and syntactical structures of the English language.

The goal of *Reading Comprehension 1–3* is to teach students to use all three levels of comprehension independently and appropriately. Students move through the three levels of comprehension while organizing and extending text information into a graphic organizer. These graphic organizers help students find meaning in text and help develop consistent frameworks for acquiring, integrating, and analyzing information from literature. The teacher models the skill the first time, but through the use of reciprocal teaching methods, the students can also act as the facilitator as they summarize, generate questions, clarify, and predict with their peers.

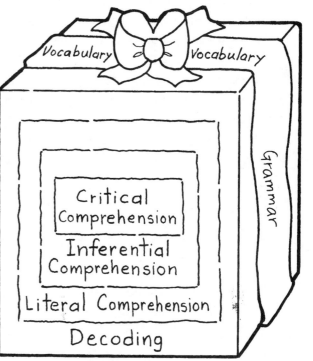

The Layers of Reading Comprehension

In order to determine the most successful way to teach comprehension, it is important to understand what reading really is. Think of reading comprehension as a package wrapped in layers. The first large outside box is **decoding.** Explicit instruction on phonics and phonemic awareness is necessary in order to unwrap this first layer. Inside the decoding box is the next layer of reading: **literal comprehension.** At this level, a reader is able to answer simple recall questions, such as *Who? What? Where?* and *Which?* For example, read the following passage and answer the literal comprehension questions.

Trabe Flemmens
In the yatz, the trabe flemmens were gribbing glunky libbles into a planky dint. Zazle glained into the dint and was sopped with glunky libbles. The trabe flemmens vimmed and vimmed.

1. Where were the trabe flemmens?
2. What were the trabe flemmens gribbing?
3. Who glained into the dint?

The passage may seem like nonsense, but knowledge of decoding skills enables a reader to read the passage. The ease with which the literal comprehension questions can be answered is directly related to fluency and the ability to remember information from the text. Most students develop this type of story comprehension early on in their education. Teaching this type of comprehension tends to be just a matter of focusing on certain points in the text and giving strategies to aid in the recall of information. This passage demonstrates that it is possible for a reader to demonstrate literal comprehension without any true understanding of the message in the text.

True understanding is related to the next layer of reading: **inferential comprehension.** At this level, syntax, vocabulary, grammar, and language structure play an important role. Inferential comprehension also involves the reader's ability to integrate the literal information of the text with his or her own prior knowledge. For example, answering inferential types of questions about the Trabe Flemmens passage may prove more difficult.

4. How did the trabe flemmens feel about glaining in the libbles?
5. How would you describe Zazle?
6. Why would the trabe flemmens grib the libbles?

The Layers of Reading Comprehension

Another good example of inferential comprehension is demonstrated with the following passage:

> Every year, Tony takes his baby for a checkup. When he arrives, he checks in and usually has to wait to be seen. There are many others waiting and it can get very noisy. He hears screeching, banging, and the beeping of machines. When it is finally his turn to see the specialist, Tony expresses some of his concerns. Tony's baby has been sputtering and making other strange noises. The specialist examines Tony's pride and joy carefully. The specialist recommends that Tony monitor his baby's fluid levels.

Interpreting what is going on in the passage is really difficult. Many readers think that the character is taking his child to the doctor and others think that he is taking his car to a mechanic. A person's background, prior experience, vocabulary, and knowledge of syntactical structures directly impact the interpretation and message of the text. Most young students would miss the underlying themes and subtleties of the passage. This misinterpretation would impact accurate predicting and other conclusions made in further reading. This type of comprehension requires active engagement with the material, an ability to integrate and recall prior knowledge of a subject independently, as well as a strong grounding in English language structures.

To aid young readers in the inferential comprehension of text, students are taught to identify key elements in their literal understanding of the text. Then, they brainstorm concepts and ideas related to those elements, tapping into their prior knowledge of the world. Next, they are shown how to narrow down the brainstorming and apply it so that they can integrate what they have read and what they know. Finally, they are able to evaluate and analyze their conclusions and predictions based on what they know about language. This type of comprehension can be developed about midway through second grade or prior, if a reader's decoding and literal comprehension skills are strong.

The last box to unwrap is **critical comprehension.** A reader at this level can use the integrated information and the text to demonstrate a true understanding of the author's message through manipulation, evaluation, and extension of the story elements. For example, using the Trabe Flemmens passage once again, these are some examples of critical comprehension tasks or questions:

> 7. Imagine what Zazle may like to do in the winter. Explain and defend your ideas.
> 8. What might the trabe flemmens do if there were no libbles?

Keep in mind that each layer of comprehension does not need to be completely unwrapped before proceeding to the next layer. However, it is virtually impossible to skip a level of comprehension altogether.

How to Use This Book

Reading Comprehension 1–3 provides the materials and resources you need to assist your students as they develop their reading comprehension skills.

Unit Format

This resource contains seven units. Each unit features three lessons that progress through the three levels of comprehension: literal, inferential, and critical. A graphic organizer is provided to match each lesson skill. Each skill can be applied to a sample story found at the end of the unit, a literature book selected by the teacher, or through the use of a grade-level anthology that is part of the regular reading program. Each unit includes twelve literature suggestions that are appropriate for the focus skills. However, you may choose other texts within that genre.

Units 2–7 end with a project that connects the unit with its skills and strategies. The project may be done in conjunction with the entire unit or as a culminating event to an independent, shared, modeled, or guided reading. The unit project combines information students learned in the three lessons with a fun art and writing activity.

The first unit in this book is in a slightly different format. Rather than being genre-based, the skills in this unit can be used throughout the year and with any genre. It focuses on basic comprehension strategies that are prerequisites for many of the other genre-based units. Any grade-level appropriate literature book can be used with the first unit, but literature suggestions appear in the Book Box.

The lessons in each unit are intended to expose students to a genre, a reading skill, and a supporting graphic organizer. However, continue to provide students with the opportunity to use a blank graphic organizer as they read other literature selections at a listening center, in guided reading groups, in independent reading, or even to organize ideas in a writing center.

How to Use This Book

Lesson Format

Each of three lessons in a unit is structured to give students an opportunity to engage prior knowledge and introduce a new comprehension strategy through literature and a graphic organizer. Each lesson is divided into four parts: direct explanation, modeling, guided practice, and application. Before beginning each lesson, make a copy of the accompanying graphic organizer on a transparency. This transparency is used in either the modeling or guided practice portion of each lesson. Each lesson teaches students to apply the comprehension skill and graphic organizer to a story (either a sample story or a literature selection). A set of sample stories is provided at the end of Units 2–7. Choose and repeat sample stories or literature selections that best meet the needs of your students.

Assessments

Comprehension is an evolving process, and assessing comprehension involves many layers of observation and reflection. Rubrics offer both the student and teacher an open, yet objective, evaluation tool for this process. Rubrics allow individual interpretation, as long as it is supported by text. As opposed to question sets and quizzes, which are commonly used to evaluate comprehension, rubrics encourage refinement and extension of knowledge. Two rubrics—one for teacher use and one for student use (pages 8–9)—are provided. Both rubrics can be used to assess learning throughout each unit. The rubrics focus on the content of the graphic organizers, written responses, and unit projects.

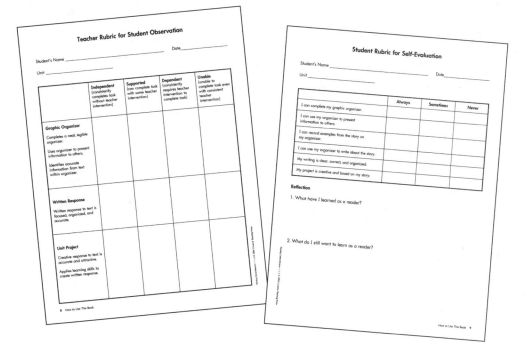

Teacher Rubric for Student Observation

Student's Name _____   Date_____

Unit _____

	Independent (consistently completes task without teacher intervention)	Supported (can complete task with some teacher intervention)	Dependent (consistently requires teacher intervention to complete task)	Unable (unable to complete task even with consistent teacher intervention)
Graphic Organizer Completes a neat, legible organizer. Uses organizer to present information to others. Identifies accurate information from text within organizer.				
Written Response Written response to text is focused, organized, and accurate.				
Unit Project Creative response to text is accurate and attractive. Applies learning skills to create written response.				

Reading Comprehension • 1–3 © 2004 Creative Teaching Press

Student Rubric for Self-Evaluation

Student's Name _____ Date _____

Unit _____

	Always	Sometimes	Never
I can complete my graphic organizer.			
I can use my organizer to present information to others.			
I can record examples from the story on my organizer.			
I can use my organizer to write about the story.			
My writing is clear, correct, and organized.			
My project is creative and based on my story.			

Reflection

1. What have I learned as a reader?

2. What do I still want to learn as a reader?

Predicting Problem and Solution

OBJECTIVES

Students will

- make predictions about a story based on a picture walk.
- identify the actual problem and solution in a story.

MATERIALS

- Predict Problem and Solution graphic organizer (page 12)
- 2 literature selections (see Book Box)
- chart paper
- blue and red markers
- overhead projector/transparency

Direct Explanation

Explain to students that they set a purpose for reading when they make predictions about a story. Predicting is making a guess about what will happen in a story. Predicting helps them comprehend what they read because they look for details in the story that either prove or change their prediction. Explain that authors use both words and pictures to tell a story. Good readers can look at the pictures to predict a story's problem before they read. They can also make predictions about how the problem will be solved. Draw a web on chart paper, and label it *Problems and Solutions*. Brainstorm problems that characters might face in a story, and use a blue marker to write them on the web. Then, for each problem, ask students to predict how the problem might be solved. Point out that there can be more than one prediction. Use a red marker to write at least two predicted solutions next to each listed problem.

Modeled Instruction

Model for students how to make a prediction based on a picture. Display the front cover of a selected book. First, name details you see in the picture. Then, model making a prediction. For example, say *I think this is a story about a boy who gets a new baby brother. I think the boy will think the new baby is the best baby in the world.* Write your prediction on the board. Take a picture walk with students. Use the pictures to model making a prediction. For example, write *I think the boy wants his new brother to go live with another family.* Next, predict a solution to solve the problem, and write it to the right of the predicted problem. As you read the next few pages, make changes to your predictions, if needed, or verify that it appears that your predictions are right so far.

Guided Practice

Display a transparency of the Predict Problem and Solution graphic organizer. Invite a volunteer to make another prediction about a problem that will arise in the book. Demonstrate where to write the prediction on the graphic organizer. Then, ask students to predict two different ways the problem might be solved. Write each predicted solution in one of the boxes to the right of the predicted problem. Read aloud the selected book. Stop periodically and ask students if the original predicted problem or solutions need to be changed based on what they have learned. After reading the book, ask students to name the actual problem and solution in the story as you write it on the graphic organizer. Ask students to review their original predictions and compare them to the actual events of the story.

Application

Choose a new literature selection for students to read on their own. Give each student a Predict Problem and Solution graphic organizer. Remind students to take a picture walk through the story and complete the "My Predictions" part of the graphic organizer. Then, after reading, have them complete the "What Really Happened?" part.

For those students who need extra practice, form a prediction for them. Then, as you read aloud, ask students to point out evidence that either proves or disproves your prediction.

To extend the lesson, have students make predictions about what is happening in magazine pictures or photographs. Then, have students write a story that solves a problem based on their prediction. Invite students to share these predictions and written solutions.

Name _____   Date _____

Predict Problem and Solution

Title of Story _____

Directions: Write your prediction about the problem and two possible solutions. After you read, write the actual problem and solution.

My Predictions

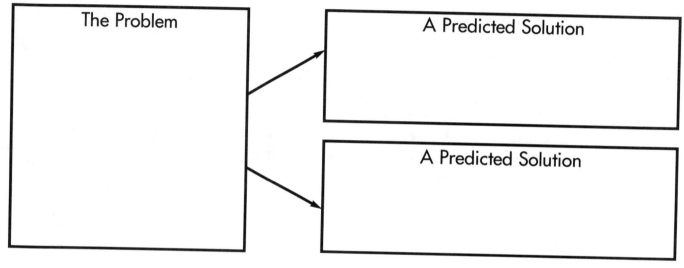

| The Problem | A Predicted Solution |
| | A Predicted Solution |

What Really Happened?

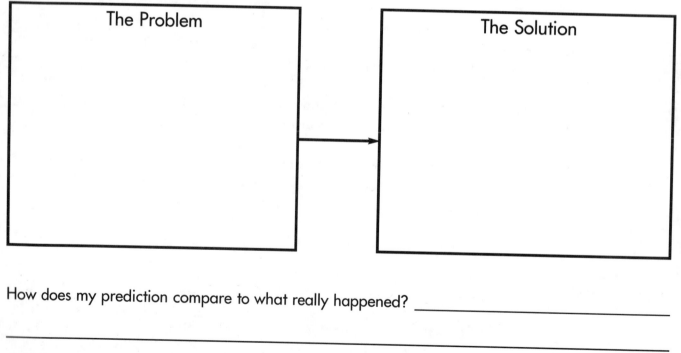

| The Problem | The Solution |

How does my prediction compare to what really happened? _____

_____

_____

Reading Comprehension • 1–3 © 2004 Creative Teaching Press

Book Box

Amazing Grace by Mary Hoffman
(Dial Books)

Big Bad Bruce by Bill Peet
(Houghton Mifflin)

Chrysanthemum by Kevin Henkes
(William Morrow & Company)

Watch Out, Ronald Morgan by
Patricia Reilly Giff (Penguin Putnam)

Questioning

OBJECTIVES

Students will

● generate statements and questions about a story.

● ask and answer questions about a story using a graphic organizer.

MATERIALS

● Questioning graphic organizer (page 15)

● 2 literature selections (see Book Box)

● index cards

Direct Explanation

Explain to students that good readers ask questions as they read a story. They ask questions about the characters, the setting, and the plot. Some of the questions will be answered directly by the book, and others can be answered by what the reader might already know. Write *Who? What? Where? Why? How?* and *What if?* on the board. Explain that these are the kinds of words that may begin their questions about a text. Display the cover of the literature selection. Ask students to describe what they see in the cover illustration. Record their statement responses on the board. Review the differences between statements and questions. Invite students to ask questions using the question words that relate to the pictures. Record their questions beside the statements.

Modeled Instruction

Model for students how to develop questions about a text based on what you know and what you want to know. For example, say *I know Gracie loves stories,* and model writing the statement on the front of an index card. Then, model what you want to know. For example, say *I want to know who Nana is,* and write on the back of the card *Who is Nana?*

Guided Practice

Read aloud the story selection. Stop reading after a few pages, and give each student a blank index card. Have students record something that they know about the story so far on one side and a question they have about the story on the other side. Invite each student to share his or her question with the class. Ask students to listen carefully to see if their question is answered by the text as you continue to read the rest of the story. After reading, guide students as they classify the questions into those directly answered by the text and those that were not. Read the questions that were answered, and invite students to provide the answer. Then, read the questions that were not answered directly by the text, and ask *Can we figure out an answer based on the pictures or what we know ourselves?* For example, say *The book never tells us who Nana is, but I can tell from the picture that Nana is much older than Grace. I also know some grandmothers are called Nana. Therefore, I think Nana is Grace's grandmother.* Explain that not all questions can be answered by the text, pictures, or our own knowledge.

Application

Give each student a Questioning graphic organizer and a new literature selection. Explain that students will read a story on their own. Ask students to read halfway through the story and stop to record three statements about what they know in the first column and three questions that they have in the second column. Ask students to complete the answers to their questions in the third column after they finish the story.

If a student has many unanswered questions, he or she may not be focusing on details in the story. Encourage students to reread or skim the text to look specifically for the answers to their questions.

To extend the lesson, encourage students to ask questions about the feelings or reasons behind an action instead of the physical characteristics of a character or setting.

Questioning

Title of Story _____

Directions: Before you read, write what you know and questions you have about the story. After you read, write the answers to your questions.

What I already know about the story	A question I have about the story	The answer to my question about the story
1.		
2.		
3.		

Making Connections

OBJECTIVES

Students will

- identify details in a story that connect to their own life.
- record story details and their personal connections on a graphic organizer.

MATERIALS

- Connect to Myself graphic organizer (page 18)
- *Miss Nelson Is Missing* by Harry Allard and James Marshall (Houghton Mifflin)
- additional literature selection (see Book Box)
- overhead projector/transparency

Direct Explanation

Explain to students that good readers are able to recall and identify parts of stories that really spark their interest. Often these story parts connect to their own lives in some way. The story part may remind a reader of something that has happened to him or her. It might include information about a hobby, sport, or talent that is shared with characters in the story. When a story reminds a reader of something in his or her own life, it is called a text connection. Invite students to identify a favorite story. Ask them to share what they liked about the story, and list these examples on the board. Then, invite students to read each example. Have individual students identify the examples that connect with something in their own lives.

Modeled Instruction

Model for students how to identify and phrase a text connection. Explain that you will read *Miss Nelson Is Missing*. As you read, you will periodically stop when you make a text connection. Begin reading the story, and model a connection for students. For example, after Miss Nelson voices concerns that she doesn't know what to do with her misbehaving students, pause and tell students *Sometimes I feel just like Miss Nelson. When my students are misbehaving, I feel like I don't know what to do.* Continue reading the story, pausing occasionally to model another text connection.

Guided Practice

Display a transparency of the Connect to Myself graphic organizer. Point out the left and right columns on the graphic organizer. Explain that the left column is for events in the story. The right column is for how someone makes a connection to that event. Read another page in *Miss Nelson Is Missing*, and ask a volunteer to make a text connection. For example, a student may identify that he or she likes the same activity as a story character. Demonstrate how to describe the story event in the left column. Then, have the volunteer give a sentence that tells how he or she connected to the event. Continue reading until students have made two more text connections.

Application

Give each student a copy of the graphic organizer and a new literature selection. Have students read the literature selection on their own. Remind them that when an event occurs in the story to which they connect, they should pause and write the event on their graphic organizer. Then, have students write how the event connects to themselves. Keep in mind that connections will reflect a wide range of reading abilities.

At the more literal level, students will stick with connections that focus on characters and personal experiences.

At a more advanced level, students can make more worldly connections and may be able to relate a problem in the story to a similar situation in real life. Students may even make connections with other texts or authors who write in a similar style.

Name _____   Date _____

Connect to Myself

Title of Story _____

Directions: Write events from the story in the left column. Write how you connect to the event in the right column.

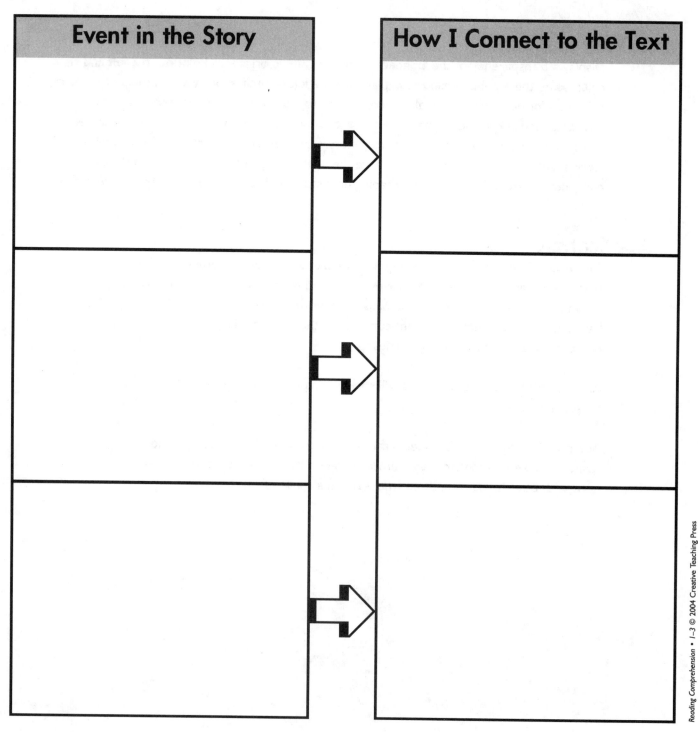

Event in the Story	How I Connect to the Text

Reading Comprehension • 1–3 © 2004 Creative Teaching Press

Identifying Character Actions and Appearance

OBJECTIVES

Students will

- identify action words and appearance words.
- describe a character based on appearance and actions.
- recall and record the actions and appearance of a character using a graphic organizer.

MATERIALS

- Look at a Character graphic organizer (page 21)
- 2 **realistic fiction** selections (see Book Box) or sample stories (pages 28–30)
- overhead projector/transparency

Direct Explanation

Explain to students that realistic fiction features stories where the characters seem real. The characters experience real-life problems similar to their own. Explain that when they read about a character, they should pay attention to how a character is described. This will help them remember details about a character and predict how a character behaves or reacts. An author uses action and appearance words to paint a clear picture about the characters in a story. Appearance words describe how a character looks. Appearance words are often adjectives. Action words signal that a character is doing something, has done something, or is about to do something. Action words are also verbs. Write *Appearance Words* and *Action Words* on the board. Invite students to brainstorm words that describe people, and write each word in the appropriate column.

Modeled Instruction

In advance, make a sketch or photocopy of a realistic fiction character the students know well, and display it. Model for students how to brainstorm appearance words by pointing to a part of the character's body and naming and writing words to the left of the body part. For example, point to the hair and write *curly*, and point to the head and write *tall*. Repeat the modeling process with action words, writing them on the right side of the body. For example, point to the feet and write *runs,* and point to the hands and write *waves*. Then, identify the words that play a part in the plot of the story, such as *The character is famous for her curly red hair.*

Guided Practice

Display a transparency of the Look at a Character graphic organizer. Choose a story to read to the class. Ask students to identify appearance or action words as they hear them in the story. Demonstrate how to record each word in the appropriate column on the graphic organizer. At the end of the story, guide students to determine those appearance or action words that impact the story in some way.

Application

Give each student a copy of the graphic organizer to complete independently or in small groups. Read aloud or have students read a new story selection and identify words that describe the appearance or actions of the main character in the story.

If students have difficulty distinguishing action and appearance words, explain that appearance words are characteristics you can see. Action words are things you can do.

To extend the lesson, encourage students to draw in details on the body outline that match the appearance words on their graphic organizer. Invite students to share and compare their completed graphic organizer.

Name _____   Date _____

Look at a Character

Title of Story _____

Name of Character _____

Directions: Write words that describe how a character looks in the left column. Write words that describe what a character does in the right column.

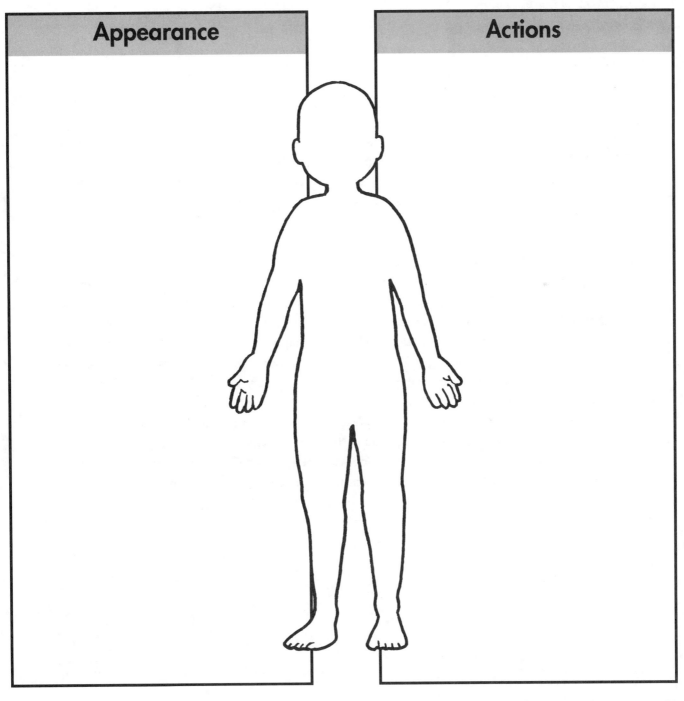

Appearance	Actions

Book Box

Inferring Traits

OBJECTIVES

Students will

- identify character traits (e.g., brave, shy, friendly, creative).
- determine actions that correspond with various traits.
- infer traits about a main character in a story using a graphic organizer.

MATERIALS

- Character Traits graphic organizer (page 24)
- Stuart's Acting Debut sample story (page 28)
- **realistic fiction** selection (see Book Box) or sample story (pages 28–30)
- overhead projector/transparency

Direct Explanation

Explain to students that good readers draw conclusions about characters based on their appearance, actions, and behavior. The characters in a story will say and do things that show a character trait. A trait is a feature that describes a character. It describes how the character feels and acts. Sometimes an author will tell us a character trait. Other times, we infer, or figure out, a character trait based on things the character says and does. By inferring traits as we read, we can make predictions about what a character might do next. We can also understand why a character acts a certain way. Draw a word web on the board, and write the word *shy* in the circle. Ask students *How can you tell if people are shy? What do they say? How do they say it? How do they act?* Write students' responses around the web. Explain that being shy is one character trait. It describes a character's personality. Ask students to name other traits. Invite volunteers to show how characters would act or what they would say if they had one of these traits.

Modeled Instruction

Display a transparency of the Character Traits graphic organizer. Read aloud the sample story Stuart's Acting Debut. After reading, write *Stuart* in the character circle on the graphic organizer. Model inferring character traits. For example, say *I think Stuart is creative.* He has a good imagination. Write *Imaginative* in a trait circle. Then, name examples from the story that prove your inference. For example, say *Stuart pretends he is different animals* or *Stuart pretends he is a frog by dressing in green and catching flies.* Point to the corresponding part of the graphic organizer as you tell students that a trait is a word to describe Stuart's personality and the example is proof in the story that shows that your inference is correct.

Guided Practice

Give each student a Character Traits graphic organizer to fill out as you complete the transparency. Guide students to complete the title and character portion of the graphic organizer. Then, ask them to write *Creative* in the first trait circle. Explain that students can use the example you used in Modeled Instruction, or they can choose a different example. Guide students to choose two more traits that describe Stuart. Remind them that they need to find examples from the story that prove that Stuart has that trait. Tell students that by rereading a story, they can look for examples. Reread the story, if necessary.

Application

Give each student a new copy of the graphic organizer to complete independently or in a small group. Read aloud a new story selection, or have students read a story selection on their own. Ask students to choose a character from the story and write the name on their graphic organizer. Then, have them choose three character traits and find an example from the story that proves the character has each trait.

If students have difficulty identifying evidence that supports a trait, have them complete a graphic organizer about themselves. Ask students to write three traits about themselves. Then, have them list events from their own life that support this trait.

To extend the lesson, have students brainstorm a list of character traits. Then, have them list the name of a well-known book or movie character that best exemplifies each trait.

Name _____ Date _____

Character Traits

Title of Story _____

Directions: Pick three traits that describe a character. Give an example from the story to support each trait.

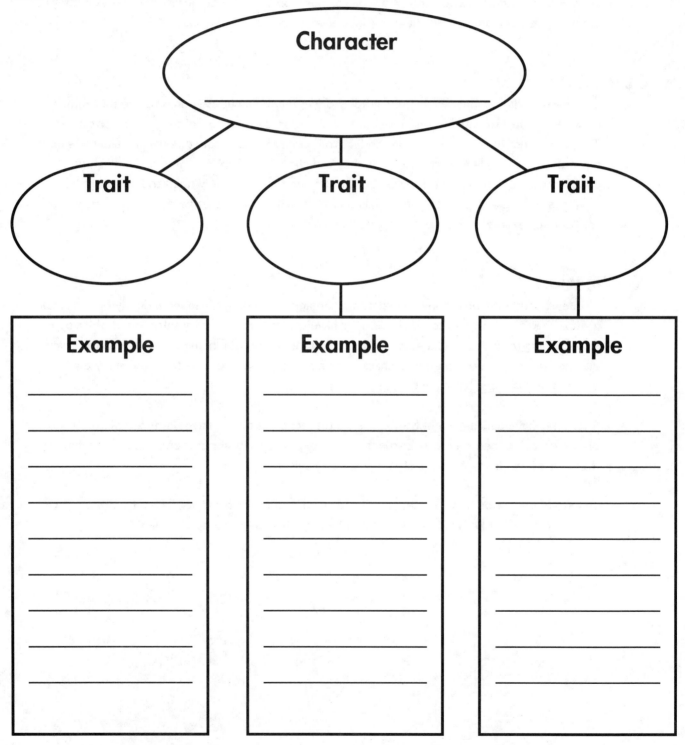

Reading Comprehension • 1–3 © 2004 Creative Teaching Press

Book Box

REALISTIC FICTION

Brave Irene by William Steig (Farrar, Straus & Giroux)

Grandpa's Face by Eloise Greenfield (Putnam)

Miss Rumphius by Barbara Cooney (Picture Puffins)

Ruby the Copycat by Peggy Rathman (Scholastic)

Comparing and Contrasting Characters

OBJECTIVES

Students will

- identify traits of two characters.
- compare and contrast the traits between two characters using a Venn diagram.
- draw conclusions about the compatibility of two characters.

MATERIALS

- Compare Characters Venn diagram (page 27)
- **realistic fiction** selection (see Book Box) or sample story (pages 28–30)
- chart paper
- colored markers
- overhead projector/transparency

Direct Explanation

Explain to students that good readers compare and contrast characters in stories with other characters. Sometimes good readers even compare and contrast a character to themselves. This connects a reader to characters in the story. It also makes the reader want to read on to find out what happens to the character. Draw an outline that represents yourself on a piece of chart paper. Invite students to help you make a character web by adding information about your appearance, your actions, and your personality traits. Write each type of information in a different color of marker.

Modeled Instruction

Ask students to help you complete a character web for a character from a story, similar to the one created for you, on another piece of chart paper. Once the second character web is complete, model comparing yourself to the other character. For example, say *I paint pictures. Miss Rumphius paints pictures, too.* Continue modeling with other similarities. Then, model contrasting yourself to the other character. For example, say *Miss Rumphius has long gray hair. My hair is short and brown.*

Guided Practice

Display a transparency of the Compare Characters Venn diagram. Write your name above the left circle and the name of the story character above the right circle. Explain that any characteristic that is the same goes in the place where the two circles overlap. Demonstrate how to write some of the similarities from the character webs in the overlapping area. Then, tell students that any characteristic that is different goes in the circle that is under each name. Demonstrate where to write those characteristics. Once the Venn diagram is complete, guide students to write a statement of compatibility. Explain that when two people are compatible, it means they will get along because they have something in common. The more things they have in common, the more compatible they are. The fewer things they have in common, the less compatible they are. For example, write *Ruby and my teacher would probably be good friends because they both seem to be sensitive people. Ruby became sad when her teacher scolded her and my teacher often becomes sad when one of us hurts a classmate's feelings.* Encourage students to include evidence from the story that supports their statements.

Application

Choose a new literature selection or story for students to read on their own. Give each student a Compare Characters Venn diagram. Ask students to compare themselves to one of the characters in the story or compare two characters within the story.

For those students who need additional assistance, have them complete a Compare Characters Venn diagram for themselves and a friend.

To extend the lesson, have students complete a Compare Characters Venn diagram for two characters that seem quite different. Challenge them to carefully examine these two different characters and find similarities to add to their chart. Have students share their completed chart with the class.

Compare Characters

Directions: Complete the Venn diagram. Explain how the two characters are the same. Explain how they are different. Write a statement of compatibility.

Character 1: _____   **Character 2:** _____

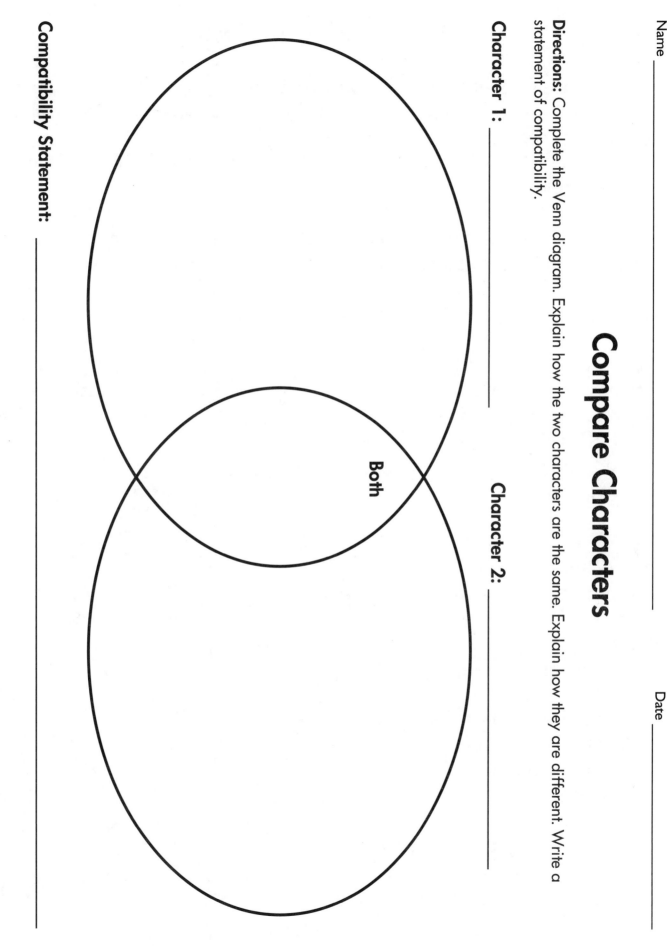

Both

Compatibility Statement: _____

Stuart's Acting Debut

Stuart is my brother. He is only six years old. Even though I am a year older, Stuart is taller than me. It is easy to see that we are brother and sister. We both have curly black hair. We both have brown eyes and our ears stick out a little bit. In one way, we are really different. Stuart likes to pretend a lot.

Sometimes Stuart acts so strange! Last week, he told me he was a bumblebee. All day long he ran around the garden. He flapped his skinny arms like wings. His black hair even made him look like a bee. When I asked him what he wanted for lunch, he answered, "Honey."

Yesterday Stuart claimed to be a bullfrog. He dressed in green clothes and hopped to the pond to try to catch flies. When I asked him why he wasn't speaking, he said, "Ribbit!" Then he smiled, showing me his two missing front teeth.

Well, today Stuart thinks he is a cat. When he wants our attention, he cries, "Meow!" For lunch he wants a can of tuna. He really made me laugh when he tried to scratch his ear with his back foot! Now he is asleep. He curled up on the couch and fell asleep, just like a cat.

Stuart may act strange, but he is always fun to watch!

Reading Comprehension • 1–3 © 2004 Creative Teaching Press

A Birthday Surprise

Jane is a second grader who lives in a large city. From her bedroom window in her family's apartment, she can see other buildings, cars, and lots of people. Her older brothers are away at college and she lives with her mom.

Today is a special day for Jane. It is her birthday. Her mom has planned a surprise party for her. She invited all of Jane's friends from school as well as some new friends Jane met last summer at camp. Jane's mom had planned to get Jane out of the house while she set up the party, so Jane's aunt came to take Jane to her own house. While she was there, Jane played with her aunt and cousins. They played games, drew pictures, and read books.

While Jane was out of the house, all of her friends arrived. When Jane walked in, everyone jumped out and yelled, "Surprise!" Jane dropped the picture she had made. At first, Jane was frightened. Then she looked around and realized that everyone she cared about was there.

There were a lot of gifts on the table. "Are those all for me?" Jane asked. In turn, each guest handed her a package. She got new games and books. She got two new T-shirts.

Finally, there was one gift left. Jane was hoping it was a brown stuffed bear she had wished for. She lifted the top off the box. A brown fuzzy face smiled up at her. Jane grinned back at the bear. It was her bear! The bear she had wanted so badly.

Jane turned to her friends and family and declared, "Thank you. This is the best birthday ever! And the best part is you are all here to spend it with me."

Mrs. Blandy

Mrs. Blandy is a first-grade teacher. Mrs. Blandy likes first grade a lot. She gets to tell stories with puppets. She teaches how to paint with fingerpaint. She sings rhymes about the alphabet. But best of all, she likes that she is taller than the first graders. She is not taller than the fifth graders. Mrs. Blandy is not very tall.

Every morning Mrs. Blandy has bus patrol. In front of the school, Mrs. Blandy waits calmly as the school bus arrives. Her bright green eyes watch for the children. She will help the younger children get to class. She will help the older children remember their homework. As the bus door opens, Mrs. Blandy greets the children with a cheery smile.

Soon Mrs. Blandy is surrounded by children. Only the top of her short blond hair can be seen over the heads of the others. The older children get off the bus. Now Mrs. Blandy cannot be seen at all. She has disappeared in a sea of children!

Suddenly, a very loud, very deep, growly voice yells, "IT IS TIME TO GO TO CLASS! PLEASE!"

The children stop. They look around. Where did that voice come from? They do not know. They do not see an adult anywhere. The children shuffle off to class.

There is Mrs. Blandy, left behind. Her hands are on her hips. She smiles. She may be small, but her mighty voice works every time!

Character Masks

Character masks are a great way to integrate all the aspects of character analysis and inference. A parade of characters is a wonderful culminating event that celebrates students' accomplishments.

MATERIALS

- file folders
- scissors
- glue
- flesh-colored construction paper
- brown grocery bags (1 for each student)
- construction paper scraps in assorted colors
- buttons, yarn, cloth
- chart paper

In advance, make "people shapes" by drawing an outline of a head, neck, and shoulders on an open file folder for each student. Cut out the people shapes. Have students trace their pattern onto flesh-colored construction paper. Ask students to cut out the people shape and glue it to a grocery bag. Show them how to place the neck at the bottom of their bag. Invite students to choose a character and decorate their mask using assorted craft materials. Remind them to think about the appearance and actions of their character as they choose decorations. Assist students as they cut out eye holes in the appropriate place and shoulder slots on the side of the bag. Invite students to wear their completed character mask as they recall the appearance, actions, and traits of their character. After each student has shared, invite volunteers to name two characters that might be compatible with one another and explain why they think this is so.

Explain to students that they will choose a character they have read about in any of the three lessons and write a line poem about the character. Write the directions shown below on chart paper. As a class, write a line poem together. Then, have students write one on their own, using the same directions. Invite students to share their completed line poem in small groups.

Sentence 1—Name the character and what story he or she is from.
Sentence 2—Tell about the character's appearance.
Sentence 3—Tell about the character's actions.
Sentence 4—Tell about a character trait and include evidence.
Sentence 5—Compare the character to another character or yourself.
Sentence 6—Contrast the character with another character or yourself.
Sentence 7—Name another character or person who would be compatible with your character and explain why.

Book Box

MYSTERY

Berenstain Bears and the Missing Honey by Stan and Jan Berenstain (Random House)

Mud Flat Mystery by James Stevenson (HarperCollins)

The Mystery of the Missing Red Mitten by Steven Kellogg (Penguin Putnam)

Nate the Great by Marjorie Weinman Sharmat (Bantam Doubleday Dell)

Identifying Setting Elements

OBJECTIVES

Students will

● identify and classify words that describe the setting.

● use a graphic organizer to record and classify words that authors use to identify the setting.

MATERIALS

● Setting Web graphic organizer (page 34)

● **mystery** selection (see Book Box) or sample story (pages 41–43)

● index cards

● overhead projector/transparency

Direct Explanation

Explain to the class that in mysteries the main character deals with a perplexing problem that must be solved. Often the problem involves missing items or stolen objects. The solution may require clues and detectives. The setting of a mystery often provides some of the clues needed to solve the problem. Explain that the setting of a story is where a story takes place. Write these headings on the board: *Place/Objects*, *Season/Weather*, and *Time/Date*. Ask students to brainstorm words that describe places or objects that might be part of a mystery. Record their responses under the "Place/Objects" heading. Then, explain that another part of the setting is when a story takes place. Brainstorm with students time or date words, and write them under the "Time/Date" heading. Explain that the third kind of setting words describe the weather or the season when a story takes place. Brainstorm these kinds of words, and record them under the "Season/Weather" heading. Ask students to look for these kinds of setting words as they read mysteries.

Modeled Instruction

In advance, write these phrases on index cards: *rain clouds filled the sky, just past midnight, a sealed wooden box, a locked door, a thick fog, a haunted house, a damp dark cave, a twisting forest path, Halloween night, early in the morning, a shadow behind a curtain, an empty theater.* Give each card to a volunteer. Explain that each of these phrases describes a setting that might be found in a mystery. Model for students how to classify the setting words and how to describe why these words might be in a mystery. For example, say *"Rain clouds filled the sky" are words that describe the weather. I might read this in a mystery because dark clouds are scary. Sometimes they are a sign that a thunderstorm will happen soon and that kind of storm is really scary.*

Guided Practice

Display a transparency of the Setting Web graphic organizer. Point out that the graphic organizer is divided into three categories. Model where to write *rain clouds filled the sky* under "Season/Weather." Then, invite a volunteer to hold up his or her card. Read the card aloud, and ask the student to tell why this phrase might be found in a mystery book and to which category it belongs. Record the phrase on the graphic organizer. Repeat this activity until you have recorded all the phrases on the graphic organizer.

Application

Choose a mystery or sample story to share with the class. As you read, ask students to listen for words that describe the setting. Pause occasionally, and ask students to share the words. Write them on the board. After reading the story, give each student a Setting Web graphic organizer. Divide the class into small groups. Have group members work together to record the setting words and phrases from the board. Have groups share their organizers with the class.

For students who have trouble identifying or classifying setting words, read the story first. Then, ask questions to help them locate setting words and phrases. For example, ask *What time is it in the story? What time of the year is it? How can you tell?*

To extend the lesson, have students read a mystery and identify setting words. Have them determine which words add to the mystery of the story and which ones do not.

Setting Web

Title of Story _____

Directions: Write in the boxes the words that describe each part of the setting of the mystery.

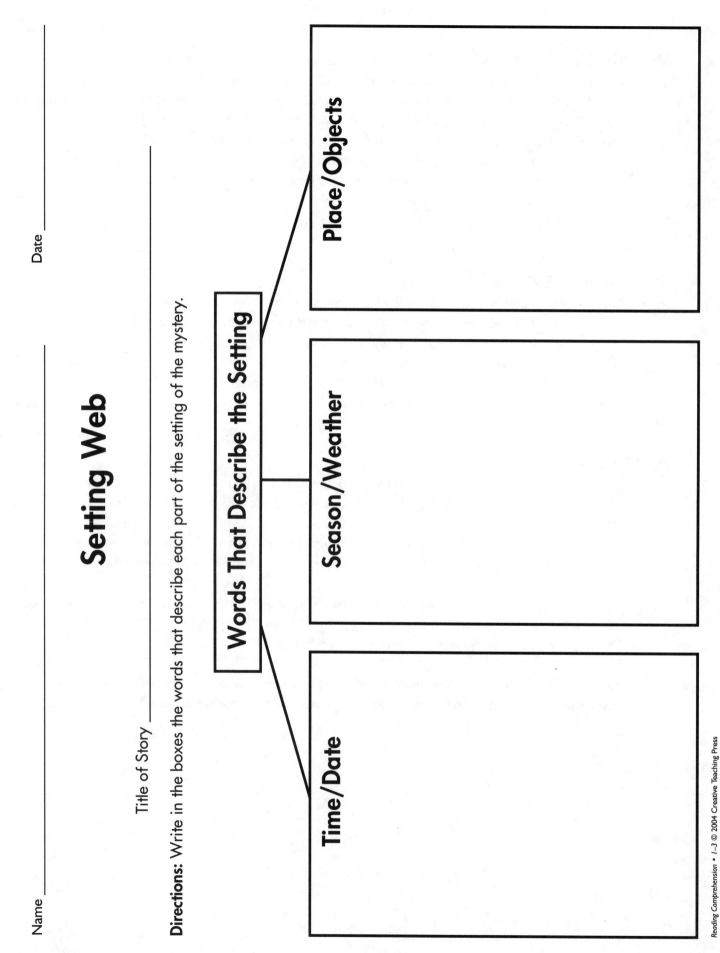

Words That Describe the Setting

Place/Objects

Season/Weather

Time/Date

Visualizing the Setting

OBJECTIVES

Students will

- identify words the author uses to describe the setting.
- use prior knowledge and story clues to visualize details about the setting.

Direct Explanation

Explain to students that sometimes an author does not tell readers every detail of the setting in a story. Sometimes good readers use what they already know to figure out what other features are a part of the setting. Good readers visualize, or picture in their mind, details about the setting. Explain that an author will use certain words to describe the setting. A reader assumes that other details are a part of that setting. Write the word *bedroom* on the board. Tell students to visualize a bedroom of a child their age. Explain that all they know is the story will take place in a bedroom. Ask students *If we know the story takes place in a child's bedroom, what other things do you picture in your mind?* Write student responses (e.g., *bed, pillow, toys, clothes*) on the board. Encourage students to use general categories, like toys, rather than brand-name items. Point out that certain features, such as carpeted or wooden floors, cannot be determined unless they find more clues in the story. Remind students that clues can be found in the text or the pictures of a story.

Modeled Instruction

Model for students how to visualize setting details. Say *I am picturing the bedroom of a child in my mind. In my mind, I see a small bed with two pillows. There is a doll on the bed. The floor has carpet on it. There is a bookcase filled with books. There are some toys and clothes on the floor.* Then, explain *I am picturing these details because this is what my room looked like when I was that age. I am using what I already know to predict what might be in the bedroom.* Explain to students that they can visualize details of a setting based on what they already know about similar settings.

Guided Practice

Display a transparency of the Missing Parts graphic organizer. Tell students that together you will read the book *There's a Nightmare in My Closet.* Ask *Just from the author's title, what do we know about the setting?* Show students where to write *closet* under the top half of the "Place/Objects" column. Then, show students the cover of the book. Ask them if they can add anything else to the graphic organizer based on the picture (e.g., dresser, toys, tricycle). Then, ask *Is there anything you can figure out about the setting based on what we have learned so far?* Point out that the story probably takes place in the boy's bedroom. Write *bedroom* in the second half of the graphic organizer under "Place/Objects." Invite volunteers to explain what clues helped you figure out the setting is in the boy's bedroom. Read aloud the story. Then, invite students to identify words to place in the "Time/Date" column and the "Season/Weather" column. Explain that it is all right if there are no words to place in the top half. Then, using the pictures and word clues, invite students to infer details of the setting and add these details to the bottom half of the graphic organizer. Encourage students to identify the clues they used to infer these details.

Application

Give each student a Missing Parts graphic organizer. Explain to students that they will read a story on their own. First, have students find and write words the author uses to describe the setting. Then, ask students to write more details based on clues from the story. Invite students to share their completed graphic organizer with the class and share the clues they used to visualize the setting.

If students have difficulty finding and using clues, read a sentence that gives some setting clues such as *When I was safe in bed, I'd peek . . . sometimes.* Ask students to identify any setting words (bed). Then, ask leading questions such as *What do you do to be safe in bed?* (pull the covers up high) *What object does that clue give you about the setting?* (there must be covers on the bed)

To extend the lesson, have students draw a picture of the setting using the information from their graphic organizer. Encourage them to include as many details as possible.

Missing Parts

Title of Story _____

Directions: In the top half, list words the author uses to describe the setting. In the bottom half, write what you can visualize about the setting.

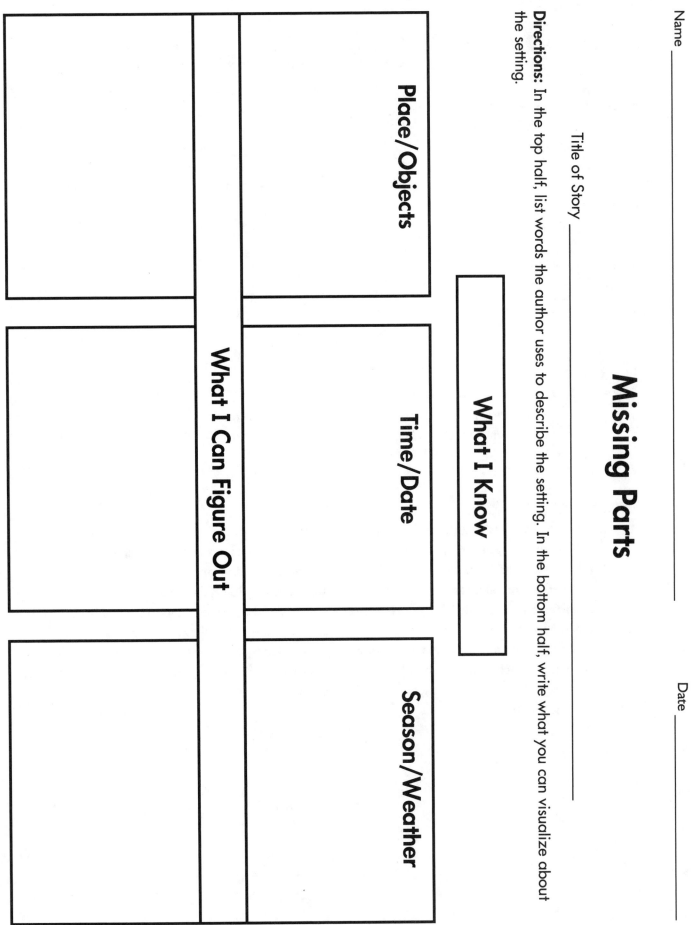

Place/Objects

Time/Date

Season/Weather

What I Know

What I Can Figure Out

Altering the Setting

OBJECTIVES

Students will

- recall elements of a familiar story.
- brainstorm how story elements might change if the setting were altered.
- determine changes to story elements by altering the setting using a graphic organizer.

MATERIALS

- Alter the Setting graphic organizer (page 40)
- **mystery** selection (see Book Box) or sample story (pages 41–43)
- overhead projector/transparency

Direct Explanation

Explain to students that the setting is an important element of the story. Often, the setting plays a role in the story and if the setting is changed, other elements in the story change too. Review with students the story elements of character, problem, solution, and setting. Have students recall these story elements for a familiar story such as Little Red Riding Hood. Make a column for each element on the board, and write students' responses under the correct headings. Invite students to explain how the setting of the forest affects the other elements. For example, a woodsman and wolf are found in the forest, or Little Red Riding Hood wears her hood to keep warm in the cool forest. Then, ask students to imagine that instead of the forest, the setting for the story is a warm sunny beach. Ask *How would changing the setting to the beach affect the other parts of the story?*

Modeled Instruction

Model for students how a change in setting affects story elements. Start with a character. For example, Red Riding Hood wouldn't wear a hot, hooded cloak on the beach. She wouldn't have to travel through the dark scary woods to bring food to her grandmother. Wolves don't live at the beach. Then, give students an example of how the setting might be different. For example, say *Instead of walking through the forest, Little Red Riding Hood must visit her grandmother across the water. She travels in a boat to bring her grandmother fresh fruit and fish. Instead of a wolf, a shark might be out to get Little Red Riding Hood.*

Guided Practice

Invite students to continue giving examples of how each element of the Little Red Riding Hood story changes to fit the new setting. Then, display a transparency of the Alter the Setting graphic organizer. Demonstrate where to write the story title and the elements of the story that students recalled earlier. Brainstorm and record on the board a list of various setting possibilities. Have students pick a new setting. Invite volunteers to describe the new setting, and write these details in the appropriate box. Then, ask students to tell how the characters, the problem, and the solution would change to fit the new setting. Demonstrate where the information should be written on the graphic organizer.

Application

Give each student a copy of the graphic organizer to complete independently or in a small group. Read aloud a new story selection, or have students read a story selection on their own. Ask students to write the story elements on the top half of the graphic organizer as they are now in the story. Then, have them select an alternate setting from the list they previously brainstormed. Ask them to write on their graphic organizer how each element changes with the altered setting. Invite students to share their completed graphic organizer with the class.

For students who are having difficulty, first select a new setting and list its people, animals, and objects. Then, have them identify the characters from the story that would not be found in the new setting and choose a replacement character or object from their list.

To extend the lesson, have students use their graphic organizer to write or tell a new version of the story using the new setting. Have them share their new version with the class.

Alter the Setting

Title of Story _____

Directions: Write the information for each element in the top half of the graphic organizer. Pick a new setting and describe it. Then write how each of the story elements changes in the bottom half.

Old Setting	Characters	Problem	Solution
New Setting			

The Case of the Missing Lunch

It was a beautiful, sunny day and Lara brought her favorite lunch to school. She sat at her desk, watching the time. She couldn't wait until 11:30. The teacher stood in front of the chalkboard. She wrote math problems on the board for the students to solve. Lara looked at the clock. It was 11:20. "Ten more minutes," she thought.

Finally, it was time for lunch. Lara raced by the other students, past the listening center and into the locker closet. She couldn't wait to get to her sandwich, peanut butter and apple, her favorite. She had not told anyone yet because then her friends would all want some. Lara reached for her sweater first because it was a little chilly. Then she opened her lunch box.

"Hey!" Lara's mind raced. Ham and cheese! Someone had switched her sandwich.

Lara yelled, "Who took my sandwich? This was not what was in my lunch box when I left home. I don't even like ham and cheese."

All of her classmates shook their heads. No one had seen her sandwich. They did not see anyone take it either. Finally, Robert said, "Who would want peanut butter and apple, anyway?"

Lara jumped up. "You took it, Robert, and I can prove it!"

The Mystery Helper

Lisa went straight home after school. She was excited because this weekend was her father's birthday. She planned to bake a cake to surprise him. Her friends wanted her to play after school. Lisa told them that she could play tomorrow. Today was her father's birthday.

Lisa ran into the kitchen. Her father would be home at 6:00. It was 4:30 now. There was not much time to finish the cake. Could she do it? She wasn't so sure.

Lisa rolled up her sleeves. She set a mixing bowl on the counter. She opened the pantry to pull out the cake mix. The directions would tell her what else she needed. "That's funny," Lisa said to herself. "I thought the cake mix was here behind the cereal box. Now I don't see it."

Lisa moved things around. She still couldn't find the cake mix. She looked in other cabinets. She looked on the counters. Maybe she had already set it out? She even checked the refrigerator. She could not find the cake mix.

Just then, her older brother Mike walked into the kitchen. "What's wrong?" he asked when he saw Lisa's expression.

"I can't find the cake mix for Dad's birthday cake!" she cried. "And I'm running out of time."

"Are you sure you've looked everywhere?" Mike asked. At that moment, Lisa noticed the cake dish sitting on the dining room table. The cake was already baked. Swirls of rich chocolate frosting covered it.

"The cake! Who made this?" Lisa asked.

"Just a friend," replied Mike. He walked past her with a grin on his face. Lisa noticed he had a spot of chocolate on the front of his shirt.

Reading Comprehension • 1–3 © 2004 Creative Teaching Press

Just an Accident

Mr. Thatcher sat in his living room with the air conditioner on. He was reading his paper. He always liked to relax after dinner. Suddenly, there was a loud crash! A baseball crashed through the bay window. Mr. Thatcher took the ball and went outside into the hot sun. Some children were playing in the street.

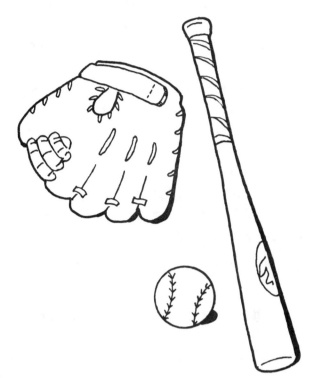

"Okay, who did it?" Mr. Thatcher asked.

"I didn't see anything," said Billy Lopez.

"Neither did I," replied Tamara Johnson.

"I heard a noise," offered Randy Johnson, "but I did not see anything."

"I was way over here, nowhere near your living room," cried Pete Townsend. "I do not even play baseball."

Mr. Thatcher knew who had done it. "How did you know the ball hit my living room window, Pete?"

Pete put his head down and kicked at a rock on the ground. "I'm sorry, Mr. Townsend. I didn't mean it. It was an accident. I missed the ball when Randy threw it to me. I will pay to get your window fixed."

Mr. Townsend felt a little sorry for Pete. "Tell you what, Pete. You do not need to pay me with money. Fall is coming soon and you can rake my leaves for the season to make up for the cost of the window."

"Really?" replied Pete. "That would be great. Thanks, Mr. Townsend. And again, I am sorry."

Dioramas

In this project, students work together or independently to make a diorama that exhibits all the details of a story setting. After students choose a story for their diorama, have them think about the place/objects, time/date, and season/weather for their setting. Remind them to include visual details for each category.

MATERIALS

- shoe box
- construction paper
- scissors
- crayons or markers

- glue
- assorted craft materials
- chart paper

Have students choose an important scene from the story. Explain to students that they will make a background inside a box. Have them trace each side of a shoe box onto white paper and cut out the tracings. Ask them to draw a background on each piece and glue the background drawings inside the box. Encourage students to use craft materials to add to the setting (e.g., aluminum foil for water, or dried grass to show a field). Have students draw objects, characters, and other setting props on construction paper. Ask them to cut out the objects and use bent tabs of paper to glue them into place inside the box. Display the completed dioramas.

Ask students to write a sensory poem that tells about their setting. Write the frame below on chart paper. Have students imagine that they are in their setting. Ask them to use the frame and their five senses to tell what they would experience in their diorama setting. Encourage them to use describing words that help other readers get a sense of what they would experience in their setting. Attach the completed sensory poems to the back of the dioramas. Invite students to share their poem as they display their diorama for the class.

Setting Sensory Poem

I am in a _____ .

I see _____ .

I hear _____ .

I smell _____ .

I touch _____ .

I taste _____ .

This place is _____ .

Book Box

FANTASY STORY

Angelina Ballerina by Katherine Holabird (Pleasant Company Publications)

Big Bad Bruce by Bill Peet (Houghton Mifflin)

Jumanji by Chris Van Allsburg (Houghton Mifflin)

Tacky the Penguin by Helen Lester (Houghton Mifflin)

Retelling the Story

OBJECTIVES

Students will

● retell main events from a story.

● determine the sequence of events from the text.

● use sequence words, such as *first, next,* and *last,* to order events.

MATERIALS

● The Order of Things graphic organizer (page 47)

● 2 **fantasy story** selections (see Book Box) or sample stories (pages 54–56)

● sentence strips

● overhead projector/transparency

Direct Explanation

In advance, write the steps below on sentence strips. Explain to students that retelling a story will help them remember what they read. Display the sentence strips out of order. Tell students that these are silly directions to make a "fire sandwich" but they are out of order. Have students assist you as you place the sentences in the correct order and explain their choices. Tell students that authors often include words that help readers remember the sequence of events such as *first, next, last, finally, after that,* and *at last.*

I take out two slices of bread.
I spread mustard on each slice.
I sprinkle chili peppers on top of the mustard.
I put the slices of bread together.
I eat my fire sandwich with a big glass of water. Yum!

Modeled Instruction

Model for students how to use sequence words as you retell the silly directions. Say each sentence in order, but add a sequence word to the beginning. For example, say *First, I take out two slices of bread. Then, I spread mustard on each slice.* Explain to students that not only do sequence words help you keep the events in order, they also help a reader or listener follow the sequence.

Guided Practice

Brainstorm with the class a list of sequence words, and list them on the board. Display a transparency of The Order of Things graphic organizer. Explain that each box is a place to write an event from a story. Point out how the arrows lead from one event to the next. Remind students to listen for sequence words as you read a story aloud. Guide students as they retell five main events from the story to complete the chart. Model how to begin each statement with a sequence word. Point out that students should only tell the most important events so the retelling doesn't get too long. Invite volunteers to read the completed graphic organizer while others check that the main events have been covered. Make changes, if necessary.

Application

Give each student a copy of the graphic organizer to complete independently or in a small group. Read aloud or have students read a new story selection. Remind them to look out for sequence words. Encourage them to use these sequence words, or the ones from the list on the board, as they write the main events in order on their graphic organizer. Have students share their completed graphic organizer.

If students have difficulty telling the events in order, have them begin by telling what happens first in the story and what happens last. Have them complete the first and last box. Then, ask them to think about what had to happen to tell the story from the beginning to the end.

To extend the lesson, have students write or tell a silly how-to story of their own, using sequence words to move from one step to the next.

Name _____ Date _____

The Order of Things

Title of Story _____

Directions: Write the title of your story. Write the main events from the story in the order they happened. Use sequence words.

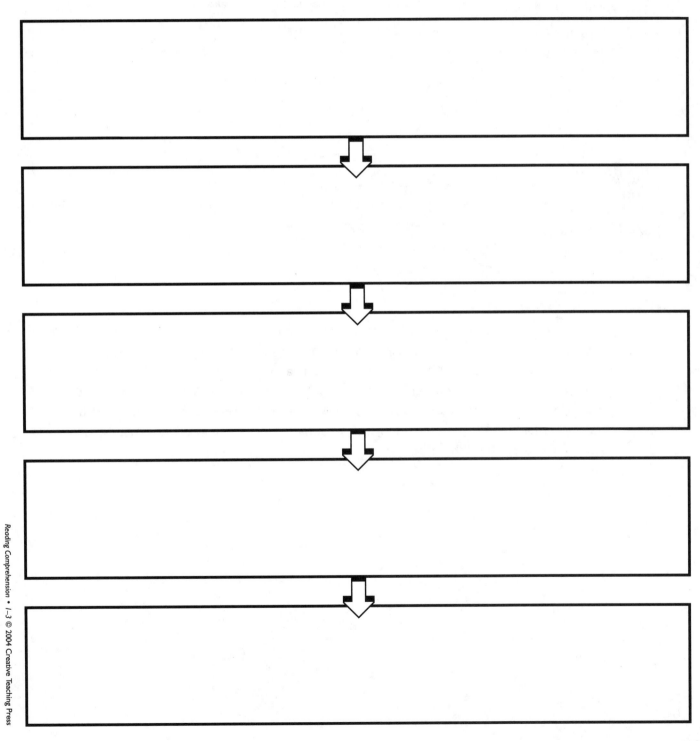

Reading Comprehension • 1–3 © 2004 Creative Teaching Press

Book Box

······················

FANTASY STORY

Alexander and the Wind-up Mouse
by Leo Lionni (Pantheon)

Julius by Angela Johnson
(Orchard Books)

Patrick's Dinosaurs by
Carol Carrick (Houghton Mifflin)

Sarah's Unicorn by Bruce Coville
and Katherine Coville (Lippencott)

Determining Fantasy and Reality

······················

OBJECTIVES

Students will

● distinguish between fantasy and reality.

● categorize story events as real or fantasy using a graphic organizer.

MATERIALS

● Reality or Fantasy graphic organizer (page 50)

● 2 **fantasy story** selections (see Book Box) or sample stories featuring animals (pages 54–56)

● pictures and illustrations of real pigs and pigs from stories

● overhead projector/transparency

Direct Explanation

Explain to students that fantasy stories are fun to read because things happen in them that could never happen in real life. Fantasy stories capture our imaginations and allow us to read about things that are unbelievable. When good readers think about real and make-believe, they analyze parts of the story and connect it to real life. Create a word web, and write *The Pig* in the center. Display pictures or illustrations of pigs. Ask students to give statements that describe these pigs: what they look like, how they act, what happens to them in stories. Write students' suggestions around the web.

Modeled Instruction

Model for students the process by which you distinguish a real fact from a "fantastic fact." First, describe some of the things you know about real pigs, including what they eat, where they live, and how they move and communicate. Then, approach one statement at a time and decide if it is reality or fantasy. For example, say *The pig tells the wolf to go away. I know this is fantasy because pigs can't talk.* Circle the statements that are fantasy.

Guided Practice

Display a transparency of the Reality or Fantasy graphic organizer. Explain to students that as they listen to a story, they will decide if an event is real or make-believe. Show students where to write the event under "Reality" on the graphic organizer if the event is real. Point out on the graphic organizer where to write the make-believe events under "Fantasy." Read a story selection. Pause at the end of passages, and ask students to name which events are real and which are make-believe. Demonstrate where to write each event on the chart.

Application

Give each student a copy of the graphic organizer to complete independently or in a small group. Read aloud or have students read a new story selection. Have students write real or make-believe statements in the appropriate column on the chart. Have students share their completed chart, explaining how they decided if an event was real or make-believe.

If students have difficulty, you may want to provide a photograph of a real animal that they can compare to the animal in the story.

To extend the lesson, give students a picture of a real animal. Ask them to consider how this animal looks and acts naturally. Then, have them tell or write a story using details and events about the animal that are make-believe.

Name _____   Date _____

Reality or Fantasy

Title of Story _____

Directions: List what you learned from the story. Write things that are make-believe in the **Fantasy** column. Write things that could really happen in the **Reality** column.

Fantasy	Reality

Reading Comprehension • 1–3 © 2004 Creative Teaching Press

Analyzing Important Events

OBJECTIVES

Students will

● identify events from a story, including the problem and solution.

● determine if events are important or unimportant to the solution using a graphic organizer.

MATERIALS

● Important and Not Important graphic organizer (page 53)
● 2 **fantasy story** selections (see Book Box) or sample stories (pages 54–56)
● index cards
● pocket chart
● overhead projector/transparency

Direct Explanation

Explain to students that good readers decide which events are important or not important to the problem and solution in a story. When good readers look carefully at story events, they will realize that some help the story move along until the problem is solved. Often, an author will give other events and details that may be interesting or entertaining, but they are not important to the problem and solution. Give each student an index card, and ask students to write one thing they have done that day since they arrived at school. Collect the cards. Tell students you want to sort the cards into two piles: those activities that are important and not important in learning how to read. Read each card, and have students help you determine if the activity is important to reading. Sort the cards into two groups on a pocket chart. Discuss with students if they agree with the placement of the cards in each group. If students disagree, invite them to share why they think a card should be moved from one group to the other.

Modeled Instruction

Model for students how to state the problem and solution. Say *The problem is that we do not always comprehend what we read. The solution is that we need to practice in order to become good readers. When I read an activity, I think about if it helps us learn to read.* Point out specific activities on the cards that show that students are practicing their reading skills.

Guided Practice

Display a transparency of the Important and Not Important graphic organizer. Read a story selection to the class. Ask students to name events that happened in the story. Write each event on the graphic organizer. Then, help students identify the problem and the solution in the story. Demonstrate where to write the problem and the solution on the graphic organizer. Read an event on the web, and guide students to determine if the event is important or not important to the problem and solution. If it is, circle the event. Continue until all the important events are circled.

Application

Give each student a copy of the graphic organizer to complete independently or in a small group. Read aloud or have students read a new story selection. Remind them to list events from the story on the web first, before they write the problem and solution. Then, have students circle the important events.

For students who are having difficulty naming events, remind them that action words often signal that a new event is happening in a story. Have them look for action words as they make their list of events.

To extend the lesson, have students think about each important event in relation to the solution. Have them rank the events in order of the most important to the least important. Invite them to explain how they determined the order.

Important and Not Important

Directions: Write events from the story on the web. Then write the problem and the solution in the story. Circle the events that were important to solving the problem.

Problem

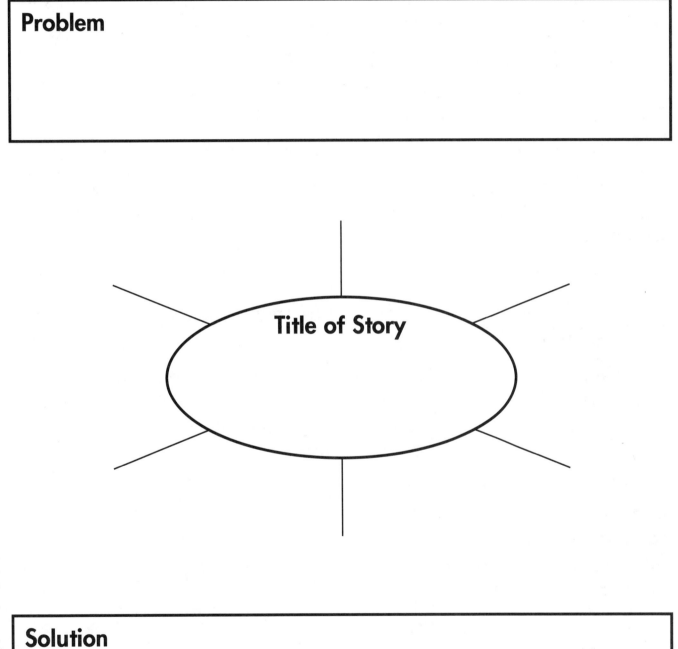

Title of Story

Solution

Benny's Carrots

Benny Bunny looked at the carrots on the produce shelf. His long ears drooped just like the carrots did. Benny did not think the carrots looked fresh. He wanted carrots for dinner. These just would not do.

"Maybe I should plant my own," Benny thought. Benny bought some carrot seed, instead of carrots.

When Benny got home, he dug the dirt by the front door of his house. He sprinkled the seeds over the ground. He patted the dirt over the seeds. He watered the seeds.

"Hooray! Tomorrow I will have carrots," said Benny.

The next day Benny stared sadly at the dirt by his door. His friend Sarah Squirrel saw him. She twitched her fluffy tail and asked, "What is wrong, Benny?"

"I planted carrot seeds yesterday, but they did not grow!" he cried.

"Oh, Benny, carrots do not grow overnight," said Sarah. "It will take many, many days."

Every day, Benny watered the seeds. Every day, Benny saw only dirt. Then, one day, Benny had a big surprise. During the night, the carrots had grown. Not just a little, but until they were big and ready to eat! Benny was so excited. Benny was so surprised!

That night, Benny asked Sarah to dinner. They had carrot soup, carrot steaks, and carrot pudding for dessert. Benny told Sarah about his amazing carrots.

"Benny, you are an amazing carrot farmer," said Sarah.

Benny just smiled and nibbled on a carrot.

A Fishy Adventure

Mark tapped carefully on the fish food box. "There you go, Goldy. A little breakfast for you."

Mark's goldfish swam to the surface of the fishbowl. She bit at the pieces of food. She wiggled her tail as if to say "thank you."

Mark smiled. He picked up his backpack. He grabbed his jacket. "Good-bye, Goldy. See you after school," he cried. He left the room.

If he had stayed a moment longer, he would have heard a voice. "Bye, Mark!" said Goldy.

Goldy swam three circles around her bowl. "What should I do today?" she wondered. She gave a great kick with her tail. She leaped up onto the rim of the bowl. Goldy balanced on the rim and looked around the room.

With a little shiver, Goldy leaped up. She tucked her tail and slid down the side of the fishbowl. Goldy slid across the papers on Mark's desk. Wham! A can of pencils fell onto the floor.

Goldy picked herself up and stood on her tail fins. She gave a little shake. Water splashed everywhere. "Oops!" she cried. Goldy continued to play. She ran here and there and everywhere. Before long, she was very tired. She was also very dry. Goldy climbed up to the top of a stack of books. With one giant leap, she landed with a splash in her fishbowl. With a sigh, Goldy drifted off to sleep.

Later, Mark returned from school. He dropped his backpack on the bed. "Hi Goldy!" he hollered. "Did you have a good day?"

Goldy opened her eyes and gave Mark a wink. She swam a circle around her bowl. Mark pulled back in surprise. Then, he noticed the water all over his desk. "Hey, why is my desk so wet?" he asked. It was almost like he expected an answer.

A Favor for a Friend

One day a giant was walking in the forest. He was looking for flowers. Suddenly, he heard a small voice cry out. "Look out! You are going to crush me!" the small voice squeaked.

The giant looked all around, then down. He saw a tiny mouse far below on the ground. "I am sorry," said the giant. "I did not see you."

The mouse replied, "I am so small and I am the same color as the ground. Everyone in my family almost gets stepped on. It happens all the time."

"I have an idea," said the giant. He plucked a shiny red leaf from a tree nearby. He folded it and tore it. He made a little vest from the bright red leaf. "If you wear this, you will be easier to see," said the giant.

"Oh! Thank you so much!" cried the mouse. He scurried off, proud of his new red vest.

That night the giant sat down to dinner by himself. He felt very alone. "I am so lonely," he said. "I wish I had someone to talk to. I wish I had someone to eat with. I really wish I had a friend."

"You do!" squeaked many little voices from the floor.

The startled giant looked down. There was the mouse in his little red vest. There were also many other mice as well. "Mr. Giant, you were so kind to me," squeaked the mouse. "Can you help my family, too? Then, we will keep you company!"

So the giant made little vests for all the mice. The mice joined the giant for dinner every night. They shared stories. They played games. They were all friends from then on.

Reading Comprehension • 1–3 © 2004 Creative Teaching Press

UNIT PROJECT Comic Strip Scrolls

Use this project to help students practice identifying main events and sequencing the events in order. Have students create pictures for a comic strip that can be unrolled to retell the important events of a story they have read.

MATERIALS

- 9" x 12" (23 cm x 30.5 cm) white drawing paper
- dowels or paper towel tubes
- tape
- watercolors and brushes
- crayons or markers
- The Order of Things graphic organizer (page 47) (optional)
- scissors
- construction paper
- strips cut from lined writing paper
- glue

Divide the class into small groups. Give each group five sheets of drawing paper, two dowels or paper towel tubes, tape, watercolors, and crayons or markers. Ask groups to choose a story they have read and discuss how they can make it into a comic strip. Invite students to plan their story with a graphic organizer, if needed. Have students consider five main events from the story that tell the problem and how it was solved. Ask them to draw a picture on a separate sheet of paper for each event.

Encourage them to use watercolors to paint a background. After the paint has dried, have them draw details of the scene. Assist students as they tape the five pictures together in order. Tape each end of the assembled strip to a dowel or tube. Roll the strip up on the right side. Have groups unroll their tube, one scene at a time, as they retell the story for the class.

For the second part of the project, cut speech bubbles from construction paper. Have groups write captions and dialogue for their comic strip scroll. Ask them to write on a strip of lined paper the event that takes place in each scene. Have them glue each strip to the bottom of its matching scene. Then, give each group several speech bubbles. Invite groups to write dialogue for the characters that appear in each scene to help retell the actions of the story. Ask them to glue the speech bubbles in place. Have groups display their finished scroll for others to read.

Collecting and Categorizing Facts

OBJECTIVES

Students will

- take notes about animal facts in a nonfiction text.
- organize the facts using a graphic organizer.

MATERIALS

- Collect and Organize Facts graphic organizer (page 60)
- 2 **nonfiction** selections (see Book Box) or sample stories (pages 67–69)
- overhead projector/transparency

Direct Explanation

Explain to students that nonfiction books tell about real things. Nonfiction books contain facts about a topic, such as an animal, a place, an idea, or a person. The information in a nonfiction book is expected to be true. A nonfiction text may have pictures with captions, charts, diagrams, definitions, a glossary, and an index which all help a reader understand the information. Explain that a nonfiction book has a main idea. The main idea is what the book is mostly about. Good readers read to find details that tell about the main idea. Display a nonfiction book about an animal. Ask students to predict what they think will be the main idea of this book, and write it on the board to begin a web. Ask students to predict the kinds of facts they might read about in the book.

Modeled Instruction

Model for students how to determine details that give facts about the animal. Say *As I read, I look for facts about the animal. I take notes by writing down facts on the web as I come across them.* Read the first page or section of the book. Retell a fact that you read, and demonstrate where to write the fact on the web. For example, say *In this paragraph, I read that spiders have eight legs. I write this fact on my word web.*

Guided Practice

Read aloud the nonfiction book or sample story. Pause after each page or section, and invite students to help you take notes about any new facts they learned. Then, display the transparency of the Collect and Organize Facts graphic organizer. Explain to students that you will organize the facts into three groups: appearance, behavior, and other interesting facts. Invite students to help you identify the facts from the web that should be placed in each group. Explain that by organizing the facts in such a way, a good reader now can visualize what the animal looks like and how the animal acts. A good reader also knows some interesting facts that make this animal unique. Organizing the facts helps a good reader remember this new information.

Application

Give each student a copy of the graphic organizer to complete independently or in a small group. Read aloud or have students read a new story selection. Remind them to pause on occasion and write any facts they learn in the appropriate column of the graphic organizer.

For students who need assistance finding the facts, consider having them create a web that includes all the facts they find on a separate piece of paper. Then, have them record these facts in the proper columns on the graphic organizer.

To extend the lesson, have students read a second nonfiction text about the same animal. Ask them to circle on the graphic organizer any facts that appear in the second source. Have students list any new facts and underline them with a crayon. Have students discuss why it might be important to use more than one book when they learn about an animal.

Collect and Organize Facts

Directions: Read about an animal. Take notes by writing each fact in the correct column.

Title of Story _____

The main idea is _____.

Appearance	Behavior	Interesting Facts

Determining Fact or Opinion

OBJECTIVES

Students will

- identify adjectives that classify statements as fact or opinion.
- classify statements as fact or opinion on a graphic organizer.
- recognize that nonfiction selections may contain facts that are not true.

MATERIALS

- Fact or Opinion graphic organizer (page 63)
- **nonfiction** selection (see Book Box) or sample story (pages 67–69)
- chart paper
- overhead projector/transparency

Direct Explanation

Explain to students that good readers distinguish between facts and opinions when they read a nonfiction text. Explain to students that a fact measures, classifies, or physically describes something in observable ways. An opinion is a statement of someone's beliefs or feelings about something. Create six to ten statements about yourself as a teacher, and write them on the board. The statements should be a mix of facts and opinions. Explain to students that certain words signal if a statement is an opinion or a fact. Opinions have words that compare or give a value to an object. Facts have words that often show measurement, describe color or features, or are proper nouns. Brainstorm with the class a list of fact and opinion words, and list them on a piece of chart paper. For example, for fact words list *three feet long, ten pounds, brown spotted fur,* and *lives in Africa.* For opinion words, list *most interesting animal, amazing, beautiful, very scary,* and *ugly.*

Modeled Instruction

Model how to decide if a statement is a fact or an opinion. Read one of the statements about yourself, and analyze if it is a fact or an opinion. For example, say *"I am a very good teacher" is an opinion because it is how I feel about myself. It might be how you feel, too. But there is no way to measure or observe this. There might be other people who do not agree with me. Therefore, this statement is an opinion. "I have brown hair" is a statement that is a fact. It is a description you can observe. Therefore, it is a fact.* Continue modeling this process with the remaining statements.

Guided Practice

Display a transparency of the Fact or Opinion graphic organizer. Model how to write the facts and opinions from the directed lesson in the proper columns. At this time, address the idea of "untrue facts." These are statements that read like a fact, but they contain incorrect information. Explain that sometimes the facts in a nonfiction book might be wrong. This happens when the author makes a mistake, or when new things are discovered that prove old ideas to be wrong. Write on the board an incorrect fact about yourself such as *I have blond hair.* Explain that this is an observable description statement, so it is a fact, but it is not correct. Explain that this statement would be considered an untrue fact.

Application

Give each student a copy of the graphic organizer to complete independently or in a small group. Read aloud or have students read a nonfiction selection about an animal. Have students list facts and opinions they find in the selection. Then, ask them to choose two facts that they think might be untrue. Have students explain why they chose these statements.

For students who have trouble telling facts from opinions, remind them that a fact would be observable and agreed upon by everyone. An opinion would not be agreed upon by all.

To extend the lesson, invite students to check facts they think are untrue in another nonfiction book. Explain that by checking facts in more than one source, a good reader can verify that a fact is more likely to be true.

Name _____ Date _____

Fact or Opinion

Name of the animal _____

Directions: Write all the facts about your animal in the first column. Then write all the opinion statements in the second column. Write two facts that you think might be "untrue facts."

Fact	Opinion

I think these two facts might not be true:

1. _____

2. _____

Reading Comprehension • 1–3 © 2004 Creative Teaching Press

Deducing the Author's Message

OBJECTIVES

Students will

- write a topic sentence that reflects the main idea of each group of details.

- deduce the author's message based on facts and opinions in a nonfiction selection.

- record main ideas, details, and the author's message on a graphic organizer.

MATERIALS

- Get the Message graphic organizer (page 66)
- The Truth about Spiders sample story (page 67)
- **nonfiction** selection (see Book Box) or sample story (pages 67–69)
- overhead projector/transparencies

Direct Explanation

In advance, make an overhead transparency of The Truth about Spiders sample story to use during the modeling and guided practice. Explain to students that authors of nonfiction give us facts about a topic. Sometimes they also give us their opinions as well. An author might clearly state exactly how he or she feels about the topic. Other times, the author does not directly say how he or she feels or what the purpose is in the selection. Good readers are able to read the facts, watch for opinions, and deduce the message the author is trying to convey. On the board, write the headings *Scary Animals* and *Pretty Animals*. Ask students to brainstorm animals that they think belong in each category. Invite students to share why they think certain creatures go in each group.

Modeled Instruction

Display The Truth about Spiders transparency. Explain that spiders are animals that people often think of as scary. Encourage students to listen carefully for details as you read aloud the selection. After reading, model for students how to identify the main idea. For example, say *This tells me facts about spiders. Even though spiders are scary, there are many helpful things they do. I think the main idea of this selection is that spiders are useful animals.*

Guided Practice

Display a transparency of the Get the Message graphic organizer. Model where to write the title of the selection. Next, write the main idea. Invite students to share details from the selection that support this main idea. In other words, have them give details that tell how spiders are useful. Then, ask *What do you think was the author's message in this selection?* Remind students that the author's message is what the author wants us to learn from the selection. Accept all contributions, and have them explain their decision. Share the idea that the author's message in this passage may be *Don't be afraid of spiders because they do many good things.*

Application

Give each student a copy of the graphic organizer to complete independently or in a small group. Read aloud or have students read a story selection. Have students write details they find in the selection on the graphic organizer. Ask them to write a sentence that tells the main idea. Then, have students write a statement that tells what they think the author's message is. Invite students to explain to a partner the information on their completed graphic organizer.

For students who have difficulty naming the author's message, ask *Why do you think the author wrote this? What did the author want you to learn? Why do you think that?*

To extend the lesson, have students identify the opinion statements and choice of words that led to their decision about the author's message.

Name _____ Date _____

Get the Message

Title of Selection _____

Directions: Write the main idea of the selection. Then write details that support this main idea.

The Main Idea

Supporting Detail

Supporting Detail

Supporting Detail

Supporting Detail

Supporting Detail

Supporting Detail

I think the author's message is . . .

The Truth about Spiders

Spiders are scary-looking creatures. A spider is an eight-legged animal. Spiders belong to a group of animals called arachnids. Spiders are not insects. Unlike insects, spiders have no wings, no antennae, and small simple eyes.

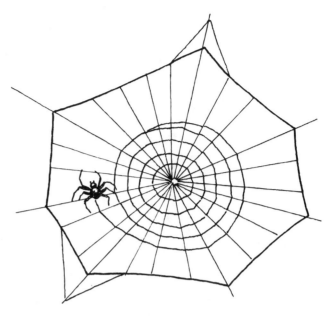

A spider's teeth are very ugly. Spiders have fangs and glands that contain poison. When a spider bites, it injects the poison. This poison is strong enough to kill insects. Some spiders can even kill small animals. However, there are very few spiders that are harmful to humans. A spider will usually only bite a human if it is harmed or threatened.

Most people think that all spiders are exactly like Charlotte from *Charlotte's Web* by E. B. White. However, spiders are not able to spell words in their webs. In fact, not all spiders even spin webs. Some live in holes in the ground or in small spaces between other objects.

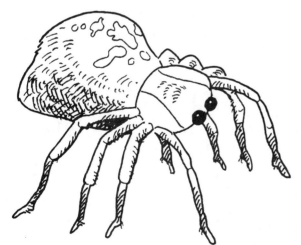

Spiders are good mothers. When a mother spider has her babies, she guards the protective cocoon. She will even carry the cocoon with her if she moves.

Spiders can be helpful to humans. They eat insects, which eat plants and crops. They also eat flies and mosquitoes, which carry diseases. Spiders are good creatures to have around.

Bats

When you think of bats, do you think of scary movies and Halloween? Bats have gotten a bad rap. They do much more good than harm. Bats are even considered a symbol of good luck in China.

Bats come in all sizes. The smallest bat is the size of a bumblebee. The largest bat has a wingspan 6 feet (1.83 meters) long! Bats usually have red, brown, or black fur. The biggest enemy of the bat is the owl.

Bats are not blind. They can see in black and white. But bats do not depend on their eyesight. Bats use echolocation to catch their food. They send a sound signal out. The signal bounces off an object and back to the bat. The bat can tell the size and location of the object by the signal that returns to it.

Bats are the only mammals that can fly. Their wings are made of skin and fur instead of feathers. Bats have four fingers and one thumb on each wing. These digits help them steer when they fly.

Bats sleep upside down in caves, in trees, and under bridges. They use their claws to hang from the surface of the cave. Bats sleep during the day and hunt at night.

Bats are mammals. That means they give birth to live babies. A bat has only one baby at a time. The mother feeds the baby milk from her own body when it is born.

Bats zip through the sky at dusk. They are helpful to farmers because they eat the insects that destroy crops. Most bats eat insects. Others eat fruit and flower nectar. There is even one kind of bat that eats blood from cows. Bats never eat blood from people!

Flying Squirrels

Whoosh! What was that creature that just flew by? It was too big to be a bird and much too fuzzy! It must be a flying squirrel.

Flying squirrels do not fly. They glide through the air like a paper airplane does. Flying squirrels have extra skin on each side of their body. This extra skin connects their front legs to their back legs. When the squirrel stretches out, its extra skin acts like wings. The squirrel leaps out from a branch. Its "wings" catch the air. The flying squirrel glides to a lower branch or the ground.

Flying squirrels have long, flattened tails. When the flying squirrel is gliding, it uses its tail like a rudder. The squirrel moves its tail from side to side. Its tail helps it steer one way or another.

Flying squirrels are nocturnal. This means they are only active at night. They have large eyes and dense, thick fur. Flying squirrels live in the hollows of trees. They eat a variety of things, including berries, nuts, dead animals, young birds, birds' eggs, and insects.

There are many different kinds of flying squirrels. Flying squirrels can be found in the forests of North America, Europe, and Asia. The North American flying squirrel is gray with a white belly. It is 9 to 14 inches (22 to 35 centimeters) long and can glide from 50 to 100 feet (15.25 to 30.5 meters). The giant flying squirrel found in Asia is much bigger. Because of its size, it can glide as far as 1,500 feet (457.5 meters).

Flying squirrels have a fascinating way to travel!

Reading Comprehension • 1–3 © 2004 Creative Teaching Press

Use this mobile report to showcase what students have learned about a particular animal.

MATERIALS

- reference materials and nonfiction books
- Collect and Organize Facts graphic organizer (page 60) (optional)
- wire hangers
- construction paper
- string

- index cards
- scissors
- tape
- crayons or markers
- lined index cards
- glue

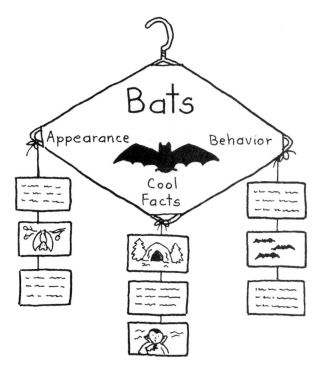

Have students choose an animal for their report. Ask them to use reference materials and nonfiction books to find out about the appearance, behavior, and other interesting facts about the animal. You may choose to have students use a Collect and Organize Facts graphic organizer to help them gather and organize their facts. Give each student a hanger, construction paper, string, and several index cards. Demonstrate how to pull on the bottom of the hanger to make a diamond shape. Have students cover their hanger with construction paper. Ask students to decorate the paper with a picture and the name of their animal. Encourage them to include details about where the animal lives. Then, ask students to draw on the index cards pictures that show details about the animal's appearance, behavior, and other interesting facts. Have students group together the related facts using string and tape. Ask them to connect the appearance cards to the left point, the behavior cards to the right point, and the interesting facts cards to the bottom point of the hanger.

Have students write on an index card a description that matches each illustration for each string of cards. Encourage students to use details so that a reader can form a good mental picture. Ask students to glue each description card to the back of the corresponding illustration card on their mobile. Invite students to write an opinion statement about the animal on the back of the hanger diamond. Hang the completed mobiles in the classroom, and invite students to read each other's mobile reports.

Book Box

BIOGRAPHY

Betsy Ross by Alexandra Wallner (Holiday House)

George Washington: Soldier, Hero, President by Justine and Ron Fontes (DK Publishing)

Marie Curie by Dana Meachen Rau (Compass Point Books)

A Picture Book of Frederick Douglass by David Adler (Holiday House)

Using Six Questions

OBJECTIVES

Students will

- identify features of a biography.
- use six question words (who, what, where, when, why, how) to find facts about a person's life.
- categorize facts using a graphic organizer.

MATERIALS

- Six Questions graphic organizer (page 73)
- Thomas Edison sample story (page 80)
- **biography** selection (see Book Box) or sample story (pages 80–82)
- chart paper
- overhead projector/transparency

Direct Explanation

Review with students that nonfiction books are books about real topics. There are no make-believe parts in nonfiction. Explain that a biography is a type of nonfiction book. A biography tells about a real person's life, times, and accomplishments. Tell students that when we read a biography, we expect to learn certain things about a person. The first thing we learn is the person's name. Write *Thomas Edison* in the center of a piece of chart paper, and circle it to begin a word web. Explain to students that they will listen to a biography about Thomas Edison. Invite them to share what they know about this person. Explain that they will ask questions to see what else they can learn from his biography.

Modeled Instruction

Model for students how to form questions using the six question words. For example, say *I think a biography about Thomas Edison will tell me who he is. My first question is "Who was he?"* Tell students that there are six important question words that can help them think of questions to ask: *who, what, where, when, why,* and *how.* Branch these six words off of "Thomas Edison" on the chart. Write your "Who" question on the word web next to "Who."

Guided Practice

Ask students to think of questions that might be answered in a biography about Thomas Edison. Invite them to show you where to write each question on the word web. Continue until you have at least one question for each question word. Display a transparency of the Six Questions graphic organizer. Explain that this organizer will help students think about questions before they read. Demonstrate where to write questions for each word on the top line. Point out that the answers to the questions will be written on the lines underneath. Read aloud the Thomas Edison sample story. Encourage students to contribute information that answers each question. Explain that sometimes it is helpful to reread parts of a nonfiction book in order to remember an answer. Reread parts of the biography as needed. If an answer cannot be found, explain that they can write another question for the question word that was answered by the text.

Application

Give each student a copy of the graphic organizer to complete independently or in a small group. Read aloud or have students read a story selection. Encourage students to write as many details as possible in their answers to the questions.

Have students who need extra assistance complete the graphic organizer for their own lives. Instead of writing out questions, have them answer the question words with whatever comes to mind. Then, ask them to give an example of a question that could be answered by their response. Explain that this same question could be asked about another person as well.

To extend the lesson, have students use the information from their graphic organizer to design an informational poster about the person in their biography.

Name _____ Date _____

Six Questions

Name of Person _____

Directions: Write a question for each question word. Answer each question after you read.

Who?	_____
	_____
	_____
What?	_____
	_____
	_____
Where?	_____
	_____
	_____
When?	_____
	_____
	_____
Why?	_____
	_____
	_____
How?	_____
	_____
	_____

BIOGRAPHY

Helen Keller: Courage in the Dark
by Johanna Hurwitz (Random House)

Laura Ingalls Wilder by
Alexandra Wallner (Holiday House)

A Picture Book of Abraham Lincoln
by David Adler (Holiday House)

Wright Brothers by Pamela Duncan
Edwards (Hyperion Books)

Sequencing with a Time Line

OBJECTIVES

Students will

- determine important events in a biography.
- sequence important events using a time line graphic organizer.

MATERIALS

- Time Line graphic organizer (page 76)
- **biography** selection (see Book Box) or sample story (pages 80–82)
- sentence strips
- overhead projector/transparency

Direct Explanation

In advance, write ten events from your own life on separate sentence strips. Include the year each event happened. Make six of the events important ones, including your date and place of birth, and other events that led to your career in teaching. Make the remaining four interesting or funny events that had nothing to do with your career choice. Explain to students that a biography is filled with events from a person's life. Some events are very important and lead to other events that come later. Other events are included because they are funny, interesting, or make the person seem just like the rest of us. However, these events are not important in that they are not why the person is famous. Ask students to brainstorm what kinds of events might be important when we think back on a person's life. Encourage students to explain their reasoning. Then, display the sentence strips you prepared. Tell students that each strip tells an event from your life.

Modeled Instruction

Model for students how you determine if an event is important or not. Hold up the strip that tells when you were born. Read aloud the strip, and say *This strip tells when I was born. That's an important event because without it, the rest of my life could not have happened.* Continue with the other strips until you have identified all the events that are important to your teaching career.

Guided Practice

Display a transparency of the Time Line graphic organizer. Demonstrate where to write the name of the person in the biography, in this case, your own name. Explain to students that a time line is a chart that shows important events of a person's life in the order that they took place. Remind students that sometimes the dates are given in a biography and they can be used to place the events in order. Other times, dates are not given and students must figure out the approximate date and order of events. Have students assist you as you place your important events strips in order. Demonstrate where to write each date and event on the time line.

Application

Give each student a copy of the graphic organizer to complete independently or in a small group. Explain that students will now read or listen to a new biography about a famous person. Read aloud or have students read a biography selection. After the story, have students think about what the person is most famous for, choose six important events from the person's life, and record them on the time line.

If students need extra assistance, have them complete a time line about their own lives.

To extend the lesson, invite students to research other important world events that took place during the lifetime of the person in their biography. Have students add these events to their time line.

Name _____ Date _____

Time Line

Directions: Begin your time line with the date of birth of your person. Write important events in the order they happened.

This is the life of _____.

Born _____
          date

      _____
          date

      _____
          date

      _____
          date

      _____
          date

      _____
          date

Reading Comprehension • 1–3 © 2004 Creative Teaching Press

BIOGRAPHY

Christopher Columbus by Stephen Krensky (Random House)

A Picture Book of Rosa Parks by David Adler (Holiday House)

A Weed Is a Flower: The Life of George Washington Carver by Aliki (Simon & Schuster)

Young Pocahantas by Anne Benjamin (Troll Communications)

Evaluating Contributions

OBJECTIVES

Students will

- recognize that a biography often tells about a person's contribution to the world.
- identify the contribution and related events of an individual's life on a graphic organizer.

MATERIALS

- Life Contributions graphic organizer (page 79)
- **biography** selection (see Book Box) or sample story (pages 80–82)
- overhead projector/transparency

Direct Explanation

Explain to students that authors write biographies about people who are famous for something they have done. The people in biographies usually made some kind of contribution to their community, their country, or the world. Explain that a contribution is something you do that gives to other people. A contribution can be an invention, a discovery, a service to others, or an act of kindness. Explain that good readers are able to determine the contribution made by a person in a biography. Good readers can also determine the events in a person's life that lead to the contribution. Have students brainstorm the names of famous people and tell what they think each person's contribution is. Then, discuss with students how each contribution has changed a community, a country, or the world. Ask if they think the change is for better or worse. Have them explain their answers.

Modeled Instruction

Model for students how to think about contributions using your own biographical information. For example, say *My contribution is that I teach young people.* Explain that you didn't just decide to become a teacher one day. Instead, many events occurred in your life that led up to your decision. Share with your students some of your life events that convinced you to become a teacher.

Guided Practice

Display a transparency of the Life Contributions graphic organizer. Demonstrate where to write your name on the organizer. Write your contribution in the appropriate box. Discuss with the class the three most important events that led to your decision to teach. Encourage students to ask you questions to help them determine the most important events. Demonstrate how to write the events in the boxes. Then, ask *How has my contribution changed my community, country, or world?* Invite students to help you write a sentence for the last question on the graphic organizer.

Application

Give each student a copy of the graphic organizer to complete independently or in a small group. Read aloud or have students read a biography selection. Remind them it might be easier to find the contribution first and then think back to the events that led up to it.

For students who have difficulty recognizing contributions, begin with an inventor whose contribution is the object he or she invented. Then, ask *How would your life be different today if this object had never been invented?*

To extend the lesson, have students analyze what contributions they have made so far in their lives. Ask them to name what kind of contribution they would like to make as an adult.

Name _____ Date _____

Life Contributions

Directions: Write the person's name and contribution. Write three events that led to the contribution. Tell how this contribution changed a community, a country, or the world.

Name of Person _____

Event 1	Event 2	Event 3

The Contribution

_____

_____

_____

_____

How has this contribution changed a community, a country, or the world? _____

_____

_____

Thomas Edison

Thomas Alva Edison was one of the greatest inventors of all time. Edison was born in Ohio on February 11, 1847. He was the seventh and last child born to Samuel and Nancy Edison.

Thomas enjoyed thinking about things, even as a young boy. He often annoyed his teachers because he asked so many questions. He was curious. He only wanted to know how things worked.

As he grew older, Thomas began doing his own experiments. Experiments cost money. He would need to earn money, so Edison got a job. In 1868, he completed his first patented invention. It was a vote-recording machine.

Thomas Edison worked a lot. He often worked all day and part of the night on his inventions. In 1870, he moved to New York City. A year later, he got married.

In 1876, Edison set up his famous laboratory in Menlo Park, New Jersey. This same year, his friend, Alexander Graham Bell, invented the telephone. Edison improved Bell's invention so it could carry speech for longer distances. In 1878, Edison patented his newest invention, the phonograph.

In 1879, Edison invented the first lightbulb. This invention made light by creating a glowing wire inside a glass bulb. It only burned for 40 hours. Now people no longer needed to use candles and lanterns to see in the dark. This new invention quickly made its way into people's homes. It was a very practical invention. It was much safer, too.

Thomas Edison died on October 18, 1931. Although he made over 1,000 inventions, it is the lightbulb for which he is best remembered. When you flip on a light switch, think of Thomas Edison.

Harriet Tubman

African American Harriet Ross Tubman was born sometime around 1820 on a plantation in Maryland. Her parents were slaves. When she was young, she was called Araminta Ross. She later adopted her mother's name, Harriet, when she was older.

Harriet went to work when she was only five years old as a maid and a children's nurse. When she was twelve years old, she went to work in the fields. A year later, she was hit on the head with a heavy weight. This injury caused her to have blackouts throughout the rest of her life.

In 1844, she got married. John Tubman became her husband. John was a free man. Harriet was still considered a slave, but her master let her live with her husband. When the owner of the plantation died, rumors started that the property and slaves would be sold. So, in 1849, Harriet fled to the North and freedom. Her husband did not go with her.

In the North, Harriet joined other people who were fighting against slavery. She decided to become a conductor on the Underground Railroad. This was a group that helped slaves escape to freedom in the North. Harriet made her first rescue trip in 1850. She brought back her sister and her sister's two children. In 1851, Harriet rescued her brother. A year later, she was able to bring her parents to freedom, too.

Harriet brought over 300 slaves to freedom during her lifetime. She was always in danger of capture or punishment. Harriet used disguises and changed her route often to keep her tracks hidden.

In 1861, when the Civil War began, Harriet worked as a nurse, scout, and spy for the Union Army. She helped prepare food for the African American troops.

During her lifetime, Harriet Tubman worked hard to improve the lives of African Americans. When she died in 1913, Harriet was mourned by all who had been inspired by her good works.

Walt Disney

Walter Elias Disney was born in Chicago, Illinois, in 1901. As a child, Walt always enjoyed drawing. When he was 16, he went to Chicago. He decided that he wanted to study art. At the age of 19, he got a job making cartoon ads for movie theaters.

In 1923, he moved to Los Angeles, California. He was interested in the movies. Walt could not afford his own studio. Instead, he drew cartoons in his garage. He liked to make his characters do funny things.

When Walt was 27, he created Mickey Mouse. This charming little mouse would become his most famous character. Within ten years, Walt created Donald Duck, Goofy, and other characters that we know so well.

At first, Disney's cartoons were very short movies. Disney decided to make a full-length animated film. He began work on *Snow White and the Seven Dwarfs.* Thousands of drawings would be needed. Disney hired a team of people to help him.

Would people watch a long cartoon? The movie was a big hit. Disney then made other classics like *Pinocchio, Bambi, Cinderella,* and *The Jungle Book.* Next, Disney wanted to try a new idea. He decided to combine live actors with cartoons. Soon, people could see *Mary Poppins* in the theater.

Walt Disney had one last idea. He wanted to create an enormous amusement park. In this park, families could enjoy themselves. He named the park after himself: Disneyland. He was pleased people could go to a place and be kids all over again.

Walter Elias Disney died in 1966. The dreams of Mr. Disney gave us a cast of characters that children, and adults, continue to enjoy.

Reading Comprehension • 1–3 © 2004 Creative Teaching Press

Cereal Box Honors

Use the Cereal Box Honors project to have students highlight and display important images and facts about the life of famous individuals.

MATERIALS

- empty cereal boxes
- white drawing paper
- scissors
- glue
- crayons or markers

In advance, cut white drawing paper to fit over the top, front, back and sides of the cereal boxes. Divide the class into pairs or small groups. Give each pair an empty cereal box, precut paper to cover the box, and glue. Ask pairs to choose a biography they have read to receive their "cereal box honors." Have students decorate the front panel with a drawing of the individual and his or her name. On the top and side panels, ask students to create illustrations that show important achievements or events from the person's life. Encourage students to use bright colors, lively designs, and large lettering to make their cereal box interesting. Have them glue the completed panels on their box.

Have pairs use the back panel of their cereal box to write information about their individual. On the left side of the panel, ask them to create a time line that gives the dates and descriptions of important events. On the right side of the panel, have students create three cartoons with captions that show and explain the individual's contribution and how the contribution has changed our community, country, or world. Ask students to glue the completed back panel on their box. Display the completed boxes. Invite students to read and enjoy each other's finished displays.

Describing Themes of a Fairy Tale

OBJECTIVES

Students will

- identify common themes in fairy tales.
- identify the importance of each theme in the plot of a fairy tale using a graphic organizer.

MATERIALS

- Themes of a Fairy Tale graphic organizer (page 86)
- 2 **fairy tale** selections (see Book Box) or sample stories (pages 93–95)
- overhead projector/transparency

Direct Explanation

Explain to students that fairy tales are stories of fiction that have many make-believe characters and events. Fairy tales have similar beginnings, endings, and characters. Sometimes, fairy tales with the same titles may have slight differences. Explain that this is because long ago, when most people could not read, stories were told instead of written down. Each time a new person told a story, he or she would change it a little bit. Explain that fairy tales differ from other stories because they have certain themes or features. Write the following list of themes on the board, and discuss each theme with the class:

faraway kingdom or time	happy ending	good against evil
magic	royalty	hero
magical creatures	wishes	occurs in 3's or 7's
magical people		

Modeled Instruction

Model how to connect a theme with a particular fairy tale. For example, say *In the story of Little Red Riding Hood, the story begins with "Once upon a time." Many fairy tales begin this way. Little Red Riding Hood is the good girl who fights against the evil wolf. The woodsman is the hero.* Explain that each of these is an example of a fairy tale theme in the story of Little Red Riding Hood.

Guided Practice

Display a transparency of the Themes of a Fairy Tale graphic organizer. Explain that as you read a fairy tale selection, students are to listen for examples of each theme. Read aloud the list of themes in the first column. Divide the class into small groups. Assign each group a theme to listen for as you read. When groups hear their assigned theme, ask them to raise their hands. Stop reading, and allow the group to restate the example. Add it to the graphic organizer in the box next to the theme. Finish reading the story. In the third column, have students rate how important each example is to the overall plot of the story as not important, somewhat important, or very important.

Application

Give each student a copy of the graphic organizer to complete independently or in a small group. Read aloud or have students read a new story selection. Encourage them to pause as they read to add examples of each theme to their graphic organizer. Have students share their completed graphic organizer.

For students who have trouble rating each theme's importance, ask them to think about how the story would change, or be confusing, if a theme were left out.

To extend the lesson, invite students to choose four fairy tale themes from the list and write or tell their own fairy tale. Encourage them to create original characters, places, and events.

Themes of a Fairy Tale

Title of Fairy Tale _____

Directions: Write an example of each theme from a fairy tale. Rate the importance of each theme to the story.

Theme	Example	Important?
1. Faraway kingdom or time		no some very
2. Magic		no some very
3. Wishes		no some very
4. Magical creatures		no some very
5. Magical people		no some very
6. Good against evil		no some very
7. Royalty		no some very
8. Hero		no some very
9. Happy ending		no some very
10. Occurs in 3's or 7's		no some very

Reading Comprehension • 1–3 © 2004 Creative Teaching Press

Analyzing the Cause of an Event

....

OBJECTIVES

Students will

● identify that an event has an effect on other events in a story.

● determine a possible cause for an event.

● record cause and effects on a graphic organizer.

MATERIALS

● Causes of an Event graphic organizer (page 89)

● a version of the fairy tale *Cinderella*

● **fairy tale** selection (see Book Box) or sample story (pages 93–95)

● overhead projector/transparency

Direct Explanation

Explain to students that good readers analyze why events happen in a story. Sometimes the author uses words like *so* or *because* to tell exactly why an event happens. Most of the time, good readers figure out from clues in the story why an event happened. Good readers try to figure out the cause of an event. Write the following sentence on the board: *Cinderella found herself dressed in rags once more.* Discuss this event from the fairy tale with the class. Ask students to suggest why this event happened, recalling what they remember from the story. Write students' suggestions on the board.

Modeled Instruction

Model for students how to use what you know to determine a possible cause. For example, say *Cinderella found herself in rags again after she had been in pretty clothes. I think the cause is that the clock had struck midnight and the magic was gone.* Invite students to retell other events from the story of Cinderella, and model how to state the cause of each event.

Guided Practice

Display a transparency of the Causes of an Event graphic organizer. Read a version of *Cinderella* to the class. Have students recall events from the story. Explain that there are many events, but they only need to choose three. Ask three volunteers to choose an event, and demonstrate where to write each event on the graphic organizer. Then, ask the class to determine a possible cause for each event. Encourage students to offer many possibilities. Then, ask them to use clues from the story to choose which one is the best cause. Write the cause next to each event.

Application

Give each student a copy of the graphic organizer to complete independently or in a small group. Read aloud or have students read a story selection. Encourage students to recall many events and then choose three that they remember details about the best. Have the class share the events and causes they recorded on their graphic organizer.

If students have difficulty identifying the cause, remind them to think about what happened in the story right before an event. Sometimes that can give a clue about the cause.

To extend the lesson, have students list three causes and predict a different event that could have happened as a result.

Causes of an Event

Title of Fairy Tale _____

Directions: Write three events from the fairy tale. Write what you think caused each event to happen.

This is the event:	I think it happened because . . .
This is the event:	I think it happened because . . .
This is the event:	I think it happened because . . .

Book Box

••••••••••••••••••••••••••••••

FAIRY TALE

••••••••••••••••••••••••••••••

The Frog Prince—Continued by Jon Scieszka (Penguin Putnam Books)

Giants Have Feelings, Too! by Alvin Granowsky (Steck Vaughn)

Goldilocks and the Three Bears by Candice Ransom (McGraw-Hill Children's Publishing)

The True Story of the Little Pigs by Jon Scieszka (Penguin Putnam Books)

Determining Perspective or Point of View

••

OBJECTIVES

Students will

● begin to identify the perspectives of main characters in a story.

● draw conclusions about how story events would change if the point of view changed.

● Point of View graphic organizer (page 92)

● **fairy tale** selection (see Book Box) or sample story (pages 93–95)

● overhead projector/transparency

Direct Explanation

Explain to students that a story is always told from someone's point of view or perspective. Sometimes it is a main character who tells the story. In other stories, it is someone watching the action that tells the story, but he or she is not a main character. In many cases, the story seems to be told by someone who can see all things and knows what characters are thinking and why they do what they do. Fairy tales are often told from this last point of view. Explain that fairy tales often have very clear ideas of who is the bad character and who is the good character. Tell students the name of a well-known fairy tale such as *The Three Little Pigs*. Ask students to name who the good characters and bad characters are in the fairy tale. Have them explain how they can tell the good from the bad.

Modeled Instruction

Model for students how the causes of an event might be different if the story were told from another character's point of view. For example, pretend you are the wolf from *The Three Little Pigs*. Say *All I wanted to do was introduce myself. Then the wind started blowing really hard. He thought I did it. I wouldn't hurt him! I am so misunderstood.* Demonstrate how to turn this point of view into a statement by writing on the board *The wolf only wanted to say "hello." He says the wind blew the house down.*

Guided Practice

Display a transparency of the Point of View graphic organizer. Write *Wolf* and *Pig's Mother* at the top of the columns. Ask students to help you brainstorm three events to write on the graphic organizer. Write each event in the center column. Invite two students to come to the front of the class and act out the events as though they are each character. Encourage them to explain why their character behaved the way he or she did. Then, have the class help you summarize their performance by writing a statement to add to the graphic organizer. Write a statement about each event from the point of view of the characters. Write each statement in the corresponding column.

Application

Give each student a copy of the graphic organizer to complete independently or in a small group. Read aloud or have students read a story selection. Tell students they need to pick two characters from the story, preferably two that are in conflict to each other. Have students share their characters' point of view with the class.

If students have difficulty telling a different point of view, have them pretend they are that character. Ask them to recall the event from the story, explaining the cause of the event as though they are the character.

To extend the lesson, have students rewrite a well-known fairy tale from the point of view from one of the less important characters in the story.

Name _____ Date _____

Point of View

Title of Fairy Tale _____

Directions: Down the center, write three events that took place in the story. Write a character's name in each box at the top of the columns. Write in the box how each event appeared from each character's point of view.

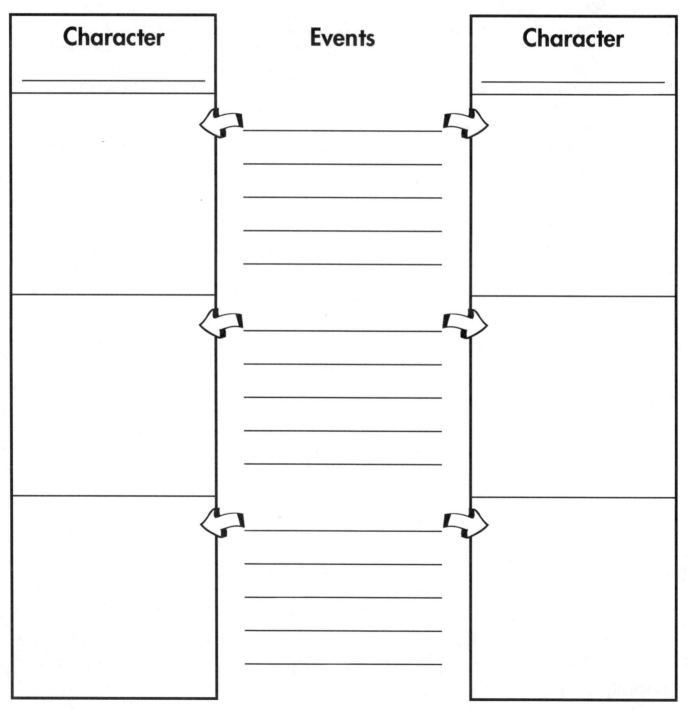

Character	Events	Character
_____		_____

Reading Comprehension • 1–3 © 2004 Creative Teaching Press

The Magic Lantern

Once upon a time, a dragon, a dove, and a troll were walking in the forest searching for berries. Suddenly, they found a magic lantern. They rubbed the lamp, and a small elf appeared. "Does this mean we each get a wish?" asked the troll.

The dragon said, "Make my neck longer. Then I can reach higher than any other dragon."

The troll said, "Make my legs taller. Then I will be taller than the other trolls."

"Make my wings wider," said the dove, "so I can fly farther than the other doves."

The elf looked at the three. He stared and stared. The dragon snorted. She did not know what the elf was waiting for. The troll grumbled. He did not know what the elf was waiting for.

The dove shook her tail feathers. She asked, "Elf, do you not grant wishes?"

"Of course, I do," cried the elf, "but not without the magic word!"

The dragon cried out, "Oh, abracadabra!" The elf shook his head.

The troll hollered out, "Sha-bing! Sha-bang!" The elf looked bored.

Then the dove's face lit up as she exclaimed, "PLEASE?"

The elf smiled broadly, waved his arms wildly, and granted each wish. Then he disappeared in a flash of light. The long-necked dragon, the tall troll, and the wide-winged dove lived happily ever after.

Oh, Those Little Pigs

Once upon a time, Mother Pig told her three little pigs to find a new home because they were just too messy. She was tired of cleaning up after them. Besides, they were old enough to find their own way in the world. So the three pigs left home.

The first little pig came across some straw. He decided to make his house out of straw. The straw was right there. It was very light to carry. He would have his house done in no time.

Further on, the second little pig came across some sticks. He decided to make his house of sticks. The sticks were right there. They were not too heavy. He would have his house done in no time.

The third pig was the smartest of them all. He knew most houses in most towns were not made of sticks or straw. They were made of bricks! He would build his house of bricks. The bricks were heavy. It would be a lot of work. He was sure it would be the best thing to do.

The pigs were living peacefully when a wolf came along. He had not seen these houses before. Perhaps the owners would have a snack for him to eat. He knocked on the door of the straw house. The pig saw it was a wolf. He ran screaming to his brother in the stick house. The wolf came to the stick house and knocked again. Both pigs ran to the brick house.

At the brick house, the wolf knocked on this third door. Meanwhile, the smartest pig took a burning stick from his fire. He snuck outside. He held the stick to the wolf's tail. With a yelp, the wolf ran away.

The three pigs lived happily in the brick house. The wolf lived happily as long as he stayed away from the pigs.

Reading Comprehension • 1–3 © 2004 Creative Teaching Press

The Master and His Student

Once upon a time, in the far, far north, lived a very smart man. This master of all things had a big, big book. It held all the knowledge of the world. The magic in this book was very powerful. Now the master also had a student. He was very foolish. The lad had been told to never look at the big book.

One day, the master went out. The student was so curious. He thought, "If only I could look in the book, I would become smarter." Then he noticed that the book was unlocked! The student opened the book. It was filled with words he did not know. The boy ran his fingers over the letters. He sounded out the words as best he could.

At once the room grew dark. A clap of thunder rolled. A genie appeared before the boy. "Give me a task!" bellowed the genie. The boy was so scared he could not talk.

"GIVE ME A TASK or I will destroy you!"

The boy was so scared that he said the first thing that came to his mind. "Water that flower," he said. He pointed to a pot on the window sill.

The genie at once brought a barrel of water. He poured it over the plant. The water filled the room. Again and again, the genie brought barrels of water. The student did not know the words to make him stop. The water rose to his knees, then his waist, and at last to his chin.

Suddenly, the master appeared. The water rushed out the open door. The master said the words to make the genie disappear. The master was very angry. But all he said was, "Learning to read, are you?"

Reading Comprehension • 1–3 © 2004 Creative Teaching Press

Fairy Tale Newspaper

Use this project to have students tell an event from a fairy tale character's point of view.

MATERIALS

- 9" x 6" (23 cm x 15 cm) white drawing paper
- crayons or markers
- lined writing paper
- chart paper
- 18" x 24" (46 cm x 61 cm) colored construction paper
- glue

Ask students to pretend they are newspaper reporters and it is their job to report a fairy tale event. Have them choose a character from a fairy tale they read to "interview." Ask students to choose an event that the character was involved in. Have them draw a picture that represents the scene of the event as though they were able to take a photograph of the event when it happened or right after it happened.

Have students write their newspaper article on lined writing paper. Ask them to use their picture of the event to tell what happened from their character's point of view. Write on chart paper *Who? What? Where? When?* and *Why?* Explain that these are the questions reporters try to cover in their articles. Remind students to check that their article answers all five questions. Divide the class into small groups. Give each group a large sheet of construction paper. Have students position each article next to the matching picture. Have them arrange and glue all the pictures and articles onto one sheet of paper. Encourage them to give their "newspaper" a name banner at the top. Display the completed newspapers.